"Everett Piper is an original. He is an intellectual, a leader and an integrity filled doer. When he talks, people listen. I intend to listen to Everett Piper. Today, we need to listen as never before. The people expect it. The times require it. And history demands it."

Frank Keating
Governor of Oklahoma
1995-2003

"Every line of my friend Dr. Everett Piper's highly original essays is filled with passion: A passion for Truth and for the Author of Truth. And they reveal his deep-seated commitment to see young minds shaped by Truth. Here is a voice that needs to be heard."

Chuck Colson
Founder
Prison Fellowship

"Everett Piper is a clear, articulate and historically-grounded futuristic thinker in an increasingly muddled, fuzzy-lined, 'everything-is-gray' world.

"Just so you'll know: he stylistically, cognitively, and perceptually stands in a long line of prophets. Prophets are always heralded. That is the good news. The bad news is that such recognition usually comes long after these prophets are dead. During their lifetimes, they are regarded as reactionaries and accused of melodrama. Why is that? Because they see what is coming before others see it. And they warn others.

"Don't assume you are going to like everything you are about to read. Some of it you may not like. But years from now, Dr. Piper will be applauded—for being right. So take his writing seriously –before it is too late. I have learned from him. So will you."

Jim Garlow, Ph.D.
New York Times Best Selling Author
Cracking Da Vinci's Code

"Everett Piper provides insight into our current culture that is understandable, beneficial, and powerfully true. The Christian community is struggling with a world that has no sense of truth and needs champions who speak to the issues of truth with intelligence and powerful conviction. Christians are still called to proclaim the message of Christ in this post-modern culture, and Everett Piper provides the tools, the insight and   ge. I highly recommend this book and

rson
ector
'exus

D1306016

"I have come to know, respect and appreciate the person, Dr. Everett Piper, and the significant leadership he has demonstrated in the greater Christian community. He has demonstrated strong leadership ability in leading Oklahoma Wesleyan University, influencing the Wesleyan Church at large. He models the type of influence Christians must have as we challenge the issues we are faced with in these changing times. I commend this book to you as one that will stretch your thinking and turn you to the source of truth, the Bible."

Jack Lynn
Founder of Clear Vision Ministries

"Dr. Piper is a man for his time: A disciplined, articulate, passionate, thoughtful, unabashed and unashamed educator of God's Truth. His writings will challenge you to search what you believe to see if it stands the Test. We are in a dangerous time in America and in desperate need of men to be Watchmen on the Wall and Declarers of Truth; Dr. Piper is such a man."

Ken Sellers, PE
Oklahomans for Sovereignty and Free Enterprise
Tulsa County GOP Executive Committee

"Everett Piper writes with an uncompromising moral boldness and with very little patience for fools, yet he manages to write winsomely, speaking the truth in love. Would that every Christian university president were this forthright and fearless."

Brandon Dutcher
Vice President for Policy
Oklahoma Council for Public Affairs

"Everett Piper has the ability to take a concept, turn it on its head and compel you to new insights. His clarion call to the pursuit of truth sounds clearly through his writings inspiring the reader to do the same."

Jo Anne Lyon
General Superintendent
The Wesleyan Church

"Everett Piper is an outstanding turnaround leader and a great thinker. He thinks broadly and incisively, and he feels deeply and passionately. His writing will not be vanilla."

Isaac Smith
District Superintendent, Dakota District
The Wesleyan Church

"Dr. Piper has postured himself as a prophetic voice with his passion for immutable truth and his precision in articulating the message. He challenges the presuppositions that distract or paralyze Christians from being potent and strategic salt and light to re-establish God's Kingdom as a primary fulcrum point in the marketplace of ideas.

"You should read this book to stem the status quo slide to mediocrity common to humanity and to sharpen your stance for God's truth."

Philip Harris
District Superintendent
Colorado/Nebraska District,
The Wesleyan Church

"Dr. Piper's incisive and theologically wise insights and his considerable writing ability make this book an excellent and readable source of information to understand the often disturbing world in which we must live out the Gospel."

Peter Jones, Ph.D.
New York Times Best Selling Author
Cracking Da Vinci's Code
Scholar-in-Residence and Adjunct Professor, Westminster Seminary

"In these essays Everett Piper has reaffirmed the heart and meaning of liberal education and its foundation of freedom in the Judeo/Christian heritage of faith."

William Adrian, Ph.D.
Provost Emeritus
Pepperdine University

"Everett Piper believes that freedom and liberty flourish within a moral context. *The Wrong Side of the Door* may be his first book but it likely won't be his last."

Mark Joseph
Columnist
FoxNews.com

"Everett Piper is an engaging and skillful communicator. It is not just a question of agreeing with him. Rather, one cannot help but be impressed, if not persuaded, by his refreshingly independent contribution to the public discourse."

Tim M. Cook
CEO
Cook Management

"Dr. Everett Piper has his finger on the pulse of present-day American culture. He is the father of teenagers and the President of Oklahoma Wesleyan University, a liberal arts Christian college—his alarm is personal. This is a book I will make sure my pastors receive! It is time for Christians to understand the issues and to stand up and be counted."

Dr. Steve Babby
District Superintendant
Pacific Southwest District
The Wesleyan Church

"Dr. Everett Piper, the president of Oklahoma Wesleyan University, has had a growing national voice as a thoroughly Christian thinker with clear insight on social, cultural, religious, and political change in America. He is both a realist and a futurist, and reveals deep concern about some of the current trends, but ultimately his optimism about the Lordship of Jesus Christ makes his work not only engaging, but uplifting and hopeful."

Kerry Kind
General Director of Education
The Wesleyan Church

WHY I'M A "LIBERAL" AND OTHER CONSERVATIVE IDEAS

Essays on

The Pride of Politics, The Arrogance of Academia, The Loss of Liberty, and The Legalism of the Left

EVERETT PIPER, PH.D.

Why I'm a "Liberal" and Other Conservative Ideas
ISBN-13: 978-1-936314-24-9
Copyright © 2010 Everett Piper, Ph.D

Published and distributed by: Camden House Books
P.O. Box 701403
Tulsa, Oklahoma 74170

Cover design: Whisner Design
Interior design: Typography Creations

Some of the anecdotal illustrations in this book are true to life and are included with the permission of the persons involved. All other illustrations are composites of real situations, and any resemblance to people living or dead, is coincidental.

For more information visit:
EverettPiper.com
PoliticalMavens.com/EverettPiper

DEDICATED TO:

Seth and Cobi

"Once you were a child. Once you knew what inquiry was for. There was a time when you asked questions because you wanted answers, and were glad when you had found them. Become that child again...Thirst was made for water; inquiry for truth."

C.S. LEWIS, THE GREAT DIVORCE

TABLE OF CONTENTS

Acknowledgments   13

Introduction   15

Part 1   CONSERVATIVE IDEAS

Chapter 1:   Why I'm a Liberal   21

Chapter 2:   Angry Mob ... Fishy Disinformation   27

Chapter 3:   Security Risk   31

Chapter 4:   Change!   35

Chapter 5:   Pride and Prejudice: It's God-Awful!   41

Chapter 6:   A Teachable Moment: Summit or Summons?   47

Chapter 7:   Are Fish Real?   51

Chapter 8:   This Medicine Makes Me Sick   55

Chapter 9:   Worldviews Have Consequences   59

Chapter 10:   Dualism, Multiplicity, Relativism...
and Frankie   63

Chapter 11:   Dorm Brothels   69

Chapter 12:   Fish on the Beach   73

Chapter 13:   Escaping the Underworld   77

Chapter 14:   Do You Really Want an Answer?   81

Chapter 15:   Cutting the Baby in Half   85

Chapter 16:   Truth and Confidence:
Being a Lifelong Learner   89

Chapter 17:   Believe!   93

Chapter 18:   A Road Paved with Good Intentions
but Bad Ideas   99

Chapter 19:   Narcissus and Echo   105

Chapter 20:   A Train to Somewhere   109

Chapter 21:   A Degree in Opinions   113

Chapter 22: The Prodigal Path of Academia   119

Chapter 23: Two Roads   123

Chapter 24: Segregation vs. Integration   127

Chapter 25: Ideas Have Consequences   131

Chapter 26: Values, Virtues, and Vacuums   135

Chapter 27: The Consequence of a Good Idea   139

Chapter 28: Thanksgiving and Praise   143

Chapter 29: Do You Believe in Evil?   147

Chapter 30: Joseph Kony's "Invisible Children"   151

Chapter 31: Playing Games   155

Chapter 32: Thank You, Dan Brown   159

Chapter 33: Defending Pullman?
             Let the Man Speak for Himself   163

Chapter 34: Brass or Clay:
             Extreme Makeover Part One   167

Chapter 35: The Island of the Dufflepuds:
             Extreme Makeover Part Two   171

Chapter 36: The Lesson of Blue   175

Chapter 37: Sins of the Right and the Left   179

Chapter 38: Orthodoxy and Orthopraxy   183

Chapter 39: Always Winter but Never Christmas   187

Part 2   A LITTLE "FREEDOM" AND FUN WITH
             Q AND A   191
Chapter 40: Single-Issue Voting: Part One   193
Chapter 41: Single-Issue Voting: Part Two   197
Chapter 42: Using Absolutes to Refute Absolutes   201
Chapter 43: Pharisees and Nonsense   205
Chapter 44: Conservative or Legalistic?   207
Chapter 45: Agnostics Among Us and In Us   209
Chapter 46: Worldview Language is too Cognitive   213
Chapter 47: Is God Knowable?   215
Chapter 48: There Is a God and Anger Proves It!   221
Chapter 49: Anger, Indignation and Bad Behavior   225
Chapter 50: Good God, Good People and Hell   231
Chapter 51: Born to Be Wild—And Gay?   235
Chapter 52: The Pastor and the Gay Gene   239

About the Author   245

ACKNOWLEDGEMENTS

SPECIAL THANKS are owed to the many who have endured my incessant wrestling with the ideas in the pages that follow. Key mentors have helped me find clarity when I needed it, precision where I lacked it and conviction where I avoided it. I am humbled by this complementary nature of the broader body of Christ. Some of its more mature members have eyes that see and ears that hear the Truth perhaps a bit sooner than the rest of us. While there are many such godly men and women whom I should affirm, I would be remiss not to mention the following few.

Chuck Colson is one of my "heroes." His defense of The Faith and his determination to be of service to the "least of these" should make even the most brazen of his ideological opponents blush with embarrassment. I am thankful for Dr. Colson's writing, his teaching, his mentoring, and most importantly for his modeling of a life that truly shows all of us what it means to be Born Again.

Jim Garlow is a friend and confidant. He is a fearless leader and a tireless worker for the Kingdom. He is also one of the most articulate spokesmen for the cause of Christ that I know.

Peter Jones is a man whose voice reminds me of the prophets of old. He is truly a "voice crying in the wilderness," and we ignore him at great peril.

Jim Chapman, probably more than anyone else, has shown me what it means to be a man of conviction. At his side, I learned what it means to stay on message if you expect anyone to share your vision, appreciate where you are going, and be willing to follow you to that end.

Roger Metcalf and the rest of the Oklahoma Wesleyan University Board of Trustees have been gracious and patient in their support of the extracurricular activities that were necessary in completing this book.

Melba Crain and Margie Knight were godsends for editing the pages that follow.

Finally, my wife Marci stands taller than all others in any line-up of godly, humble followers of Jesus Christ. She is the picture of Christ to me and to our two sons, Seth and Cobi.

INTRODUCTION

"At present we are on the outside of the world, the wrong side of the door...Some day, God willing, we shall get in."
C.S. LEWIS, *THE WEIGHT OF GLORY*

IMAGINE WITH ME, if you will, that we live in a day where we intentionally sever a man's arm from his body and then expect him to win a fight, where we pluck a woman's eyes from her head and then ask her to paint her own portrait, or where we surgically remove a child's frontal lobe and demand that she explain an algebraic formula. Imagine that we live in a world where, as C.S. Lewis warned, the elite among us actually claim it makes sense to geld the stallion and then "bid him be fruitful." Imagine that we live in a time and place where the wise and learned in our courts and classrooms and churches actually work to remove a man's soul and then expect him to stay out of hell. Such a day is upon us.

Why do I believe this? Because bad ideas breed bad behavior as surely as an acorn grows an oak or a hurricane brings a flood. Why would we expect decades of teaching sexual promiscuity in our schools to result in sexual restraint in our students? Why are we surprised at the selfishness of our culture when our schools teach self-esteem more effectively than they do mathematics, science and civics? How can we possibly think that teaching values clarification rather than moral absolutes will produce a virtuous people? Where in the annals of history is there any evidence that the subordination of one person's right to live to another person's right to choose ever resulted in the protection of every person's unalienable right to life? And, finally, why would any culture ever think that after decades of diminishing the value of marital fidelity that the same culture would then be able to mount a vigorous defense for the meaning of marriage?

This list could go on and on. The evidence is clear. All we need to do is turn on the nightly news to see the proof. When we separate fact from faith and head from heart, and when we sever belief from behavior or religion from reason, we do not usher in a day of liberty but one of licentiousness. We become "men without chests" where there is nothing but a gaping cavity in the center of our being—where instead of finding the fullness which comes from fidelity, we find the emptiness of a love affair gone bad.

Yes, we do live in such a day and time. We stand on the wrong side of the door in a room stagnant with the heavy air of our own hypocrisy. We boast of freedom and yet live in bondage to our own deception. We champion civil liberties, yet we ignore the human rights promised to us by tradition, reason and our own Constitution. We say that women should not be subjugated to the power and passions of men, but we then embrace leaders who publicly use women for their own selfish whims. We draw a line in the sand to defend the innocence of children while at the same time we enjoy "entertainment" that blurs the boundaries between our own children and predatory adults who are anything but innocent. We are indeed "people of the lie." It seems as if the road to hell is before us, and we enter its gates strutting with the confidence of an emperor with no clothes. And, when challenged, we belittle the "naïveté" of those who dare shout out of our nakedness.

Pressing our ear against the keyhole of history, we hear the voice of our forefathers saying, "Liberty is given by our Creator and slavery is constructed by man." Their lessons teach us time and again that self-evident truth is the only context for justice and freedom and that without God's objective standards as our rule and measure, men and women find innumerable ways to enslave themselves and each other while all the while waving a sanctimonious banner of personal choice and individual rights.

Ideas have consequences. Our ideas matter. They will always lead somewhere. The book that follows is simply a collection of such ideas and a discussion of the direction they lead—either toward the liberty found in that which is right and just and real, or toward the slavery and ugly hell made of our own dysfunction.

> *"All your life long you are slowly turning...either into a heavenly creature or into a hellish creature: either into [one who] is in harmony with God, ...or one that is in a state of war and hatred with God, and with its fellow creatures, and with itself. To be the one kind of creature is heaven: that is, it is joy and peace and knowledge and power [and liberty]. To be the other means madness, horror, idiocy, rage, impotence, and eternal loneliness [and slavery]. Each of us at each moment is progressing to the one state or the other."*
>
> C.S. LEWIS, *MERE CHRISTIANITY*

Part One

CONSERVATIVE IDEAS

"Ideas matter! Our ideas will either lead us to the hellish existence of the original sin where we suffer the consequences of our own arrogance or they will lead us to a heavenly joy where justice and liberty flourish, where we enjoy the freedom of living within the boundaries of what is Right and True, where we know because it is revealed to us by God, not because it is constructed by us as we seek to 'be God.'"

EVERETT PIPER
OKLAHOMA WESLEYAN UNIVERSITY
CHAPEL SERVICE, 2005

Chapter 1

WHY I'M A "LIBERAL"

WORDS MEAN SOMETHING. As human beings, we stand alone in our use of language as our primary method of communication. We debate and we argue. We make speeches and we deliver sermons. We teach lessons. We pontificate, we preach, and we proclaim. We espouse liberal and conservative agendas ad infinitum. Our "bigger ideas" are framed and defended with emotion, passion, anger and indignation. We have confidence in our words, and we resist any attempt to co-op, twist or manipulate their meaning. We defend our words with tenacity. If they deceive, we call them lies. If they embolden, we call them inspiring. If they make promises, we call them contracts. Words indeed mean something, and history shows that they have the power to build nations, define religions, inspire revolutions, and defend what is true or even hide what is false.

But in spite of such power, some words are used so frequently and frivolously that they suffer for lack of care; and as a result, their root, their origin, their intent and their purpose is lost. Words like change and choice; green and gay; left and right; toleration, integration and discrimination—even words like liberal and conservative—if left untended, can be inexplicably used to defend concepts quite contrary and, perhaps, even opposite to that of their original intent.

The best education is one that indeed liberates.

So it is with respect for the integrity of words that I offer the following premise—a suggestion that may indeed be something of a surprise to some of you: As a conservative, I believe my "liberal" credentials will stack up well with those of any of my contemporary peers in the academic, political, social or religious venues of our day.

Let me explain: I am a liberal because I believe that the best education is one that indeed liberates. It liberates us from the consequences of those things that are wrong and frees us to live within the beauty of those things that are right.

I am a liberal because of my passion for a liberal arts education—an education that is driven by the hunger for answers rather than the protection of opinions, an education that is not subject to the ebb and flow of personal agendas or political fads, an education that is not afraid to put all ideas on the table because there is confidence that in the end we will embrace what is true and discard what is false.

I am a liberal because I believe in freedom—freedom of thought and expression and the freedom to dissent from consensus. I am energized by the unapologetic pursuit of truth. Wherever it leads, I am confident in the words, "You shall know the truth, and the truth shall set you free."

I am a liberal because I believe in integration. Truth cannot be segregated into false dichotomies, but it is an integrated whole. The liberally educated person recognizes that we cannot and should not separate personal life from private life, the head from the heart, fact from faith, or belief from behavior.

I am a liberal because I believe in conservation. There are ideas that are tested by time, defended by reason, validated by experience, and confirmed by revelation; and these ideas should be conserved. We are in fact endowed by our Creator with an objective moral understanding. I believe in nature and its natural law. We do know that rape is wrong, that the Holocaust was bad, and that hatred and racism are to be reviled. Even though we cannot produce these truths in a test tube, we hold them to be self-evident laws that no human being can deny.

> *Truth cannot be segregated into false dichotomies, but it is an integrated whole.*

I am a liberal because I recognize that when we exchange the truth for a lie, we build a house of cards that will fall to mankind's inevitable temper tantrum of seeking control and power. History tells us time and time again that to deny what is right and true and embrace what is wrong and false is to fall prey to the rule of the gang or the tyranny of one. We need look no further than to the lessons of Mao, Mussolini, Stalin, Pol Pot, or Robespierre for such evidence.

I am a liberal because I believe in liberty. I believe liberty is the antithesis of slavery and slavery is the unavoidable outcome of lies: Lies about who we are as people; Lies about what is right and what is wrong; Lies about man and Lies about God.

We are endowed by our Creator with an objective moral understanding.

Here is the question I pose to you: Are we really free today or are we now becoming more and more enslaved by the constructs of the Übermensch—the superman—the power brokers, the elites, the "fittest" who have survived in the political arenas of campaigns or campuses? Are we free to live within the boundaries of justice that come from the classical liberal education—of the uni-Versity, the uni-Verities, the uni-Veritas—or are we becoming more and more bound by group think, political correctness and populous power—what M. Scott Peck calls the diabolical human mind?

You see, good education—complete education—liberal education must be grounded in the conservative respect for and

Good, liberal education is the business of pursuing Truth. It isn't about constructing opinions.

the conservation of what is immutable and right and just and real. It should seek to reclaim what has been co-opted and to reveal what has been compromised. It should be free of intimidation and should honor open inquiry and the right to dissent. It should have confidence in the measuring rod of Truth—that unalienable standard that is bigger and better than the crowd or the consensus.

Education—good, liberal education—is the business of pursuing Truth. It isn't about constructing opinions. As Martin Luther King, Jr., told us in his letter from the Birmingham jail, it is the conservation of the immutable virtues that serves as our strongest justification for our ongoing struggle for freedom, liberation, and liberty. Without such conservative ideas, I am not sure anyone can truly call themselves a liberal.

Chapter 2

ANGRY MOB, SHRILL VOICES, RIGHT-WING EXTREMISTS AND FISHY DISINFORMATION

WELL, I GUESS we all finally know where we stand. We shouldn't be confused any longer. The definition of words such as change, disinformation, angry mob, transparency, security threat, healthcare reform, and fiscal responsibility seems pretty clear now. I don't think we need to wonder any longer what our currently elected, government officials (and all their respective, unelected czars) mean when they talk about such things.

Here is a quick glossary of terms for your convenience.

Change: A vacuous term that can mean anything the current Administration and its counterparts in the DNC, UAW, ACLU, Moveon.org, ACORN, et al. want it to mean; A subjective concept without any immutable or concrete definition that can be wielded to the advantage of political power, personal whim or populace propaganda; A very efficient weapon in the hands of a demagogue or tyrant, especially when used in cooperation with a complicit media. For historical examples see Mao, Pol Pot, Stalin, Mussolini, Castro, Chavez, Robespierre, and Hitler.

Angry Mob: Any group of people that disagrees with the meaningless manipulation of the word "change" as exercised by those in power (see above). In other words, a mob is any subset of the American population comprised of people who challenge the political, social, and cultural Elites of the Beltway or the Ivy Tower on matters such as socialized healthcare, a nationalized auto industry, the bankrupting of our economy, the self-refuting nature of intolerant tolerance, the unconstitutionality of hate-crimes legislation, the intellectual lunacy of "green" economics, and all other things promulgated by the pedantic ponderings (or is that panderings?) of Al Gore.

Shrill Voice: Any voice of opposition to the message and mantra of the progressive Left. For example, when Miss California said that marriage, by any historical, legal and ecclesiastical definition has been and should continue to be between one man and one woman, she was being "shrill." When her left-of-center detractor responded by calling Miss Prejean something akin to an unintelligent, proliferate, female dog, his comments were not shrill but, rather, a righteous scolding of Miss Prejean.

Disinformation: A blog, news article, op-ed, speech, commercial, sermon, or any other form of human communication that runs contrary to the ideology of the current president of the United States or the governing majority of Congress.

Transparency: The current White House's plan to "see through" the protective wall of free speech as defined in the First Amendment and, thus, to collect a list of all the pesky purveyors of such "disinformation." This can be otherwise defined as a government attempt to "see and seize" all names of all detractors who dare to disagree with the designs and demands of a demagogue or a despot or in the present case any of the newly empowered Democratic Caucus.

Security Threat: All of those "right wing extremists" who believe in securing our national borders, fighting for our national sovereignty (i.e., veterans), defending the lives of the unborn, protecting the dignity of the infirm, preserving traditional standards of sexual morality, and upholding the rule of law as defined by the Constitution (See Janet Napolitano and the Department of Homeland Security for more detail on this matter).

Healthcare Reform: Taking a healthcare system that, by virtue of its reputation for quality, draws patients from around the world to its hospital doors and discarding this system in favor of the broken model that such patients seek to avoid in their own respective countries. It is important to remember that this reform must be "managed" by an anti-choice, pro-rationing oligarchy or said system would quickly collapse under the weight of financial insolvency.

Fiscal Responsibility: Any and all budgeting, taxing and spending as advocated and practiced by the present Administration. The antithesis is, by definition, any and all actions taken by "extremists" (see above) who seek to restrict the President and Congress in their efforts to spend and tax the American people into multi-generational economic insolvency—efforts such as, but not limited to, a Presidential budget that boasts a deficit of $1,700,000,000,000, a ledger of cumulative unfunded Social Security liabilities of $13,600,000,000,000, and a total of $85,200,000,000,000 in projected, unfunded Medicare liabilities. (Note: For the definition of Ponzi scheme see Bernie Madoff, Enron, Fannie Mae, and Freddie Mac.)

Fishy: Well, alas, I am at a loss and frankly confused. The Orwellian fog of the news has my head spinning. I guess I will simply offer the following quote from the official web page for the president of the United States and his White House staff (Linda Douglass, Director of Communications, White House Office for Health Reform) and ask you to tell me what's fishy…

"Since we can't keep track of all of them [i.e. the 'rumors' and 'disinformation' and people who perpetuate the same] here at the White House, we're asking for your help. If you get an email or see something on the web about health insurance reform that seems fishy, send it to flag@whitehouse.gov"
August 5, 2009

Chapter 3

SECURITY RISK

Response to the Director of the United States Department of Homeland Security, Janet Napolitano's issuance of an official communiqué identifying Americans who espouse "right-wing issues."

THE UNITED STATES Department of Homeland Security (DHS) just identified those U.S. citizens who are focused on "right-wing issues" as security risks!

Does anyone except me hear the voice of George Orwell echoing through the halls of our Capital, our culture, our corporations, our churches and our country right now?

Who defines what these dangerous "right-wing issues" are? Is it the Fed, the DHS, the Congress, the President, or maybe ACORN, the ACLU, NAMBLA, PETA, George Soros, Michael Moore, or even your State's governor or your local police chief? Does it concern you that someone who proudly and myopically wears the label of "Left" is now declaring that those on the "Right" are a security risk because of "extreme" and singular focus?

And by the way, what is a Right-Wing extremist? Is it someone who campaigns for pro-life legislation? Is it someone who believes in traditional standards of sexual morality? Is it that "dangerous" person who argues in the public square for lower taxes? How about the radical, "closed minded" soul who dares to call for open debate on environmental policy? In addition to these dangerous goofs, we surely must add the "right-wing loons" who think that tightening our national borders will actually be a good thing for national security? Finally, it surely is beyond question that the most dangerous people in our society are those rednecks who believe in school choice and the unalienable and self-evident reality of parental rights—Right?

Do you suppose Big Brother has decided that a person with a "right-wing" fixation on the pursuit of truth, versus the "tolerant" propagation of political fads, is a security risk?!

But what about those who focus on left-wing issues? Is socio-political relativism a security risk? How about national-izing our economy? Does that enhance or impede the security of our jobs? Does neo-Marxism compromise our freedom? Does sexual nihilism bring greater social, physical or economic security for women and children?

Then there is the question of Global Warming, or I guess now we call it "Climate Change" when weather patterns become some of the coldest in recent history. Does this blind faith and corresponding religious zeal for pantheistic Goreism (i.e., modern day Gnosticism) enhance our national security?

Finally, let's consider the post-modern aversion for a robust debate on nearly all matters that deviate from the wisdom of the Elite? Is such intellectual foreclosure a security risk?

Oh, a final question: How about those who employ ad hominem attacks on those with whom they disagree: those who label conservatives as single-issue right wingers? Is their "singular" ignorance of the elementary principles of Socratic logic a security risk? Do you feel more secure knowing that some bureaucrat or politician at the highest levels of political power can unabashedly employ non sequitur fallacies to falsely align any person on the right of a given topic with a compromise to national security? Do you feel safe knowing that this rhetorical sleight of hand (i.e., dishonesty) is actually accompanied by a straight face—or perhaps a sly grin?

This is simply incredible, and I mean this in the technical sense of the word. These worn out "politically correct" positions lack any credibility. They make no sense. They betray any elementary understanding of the basic principles of freshman-level logic. Those propagating these views are saying that people who are conservative and who disagree with the progressive mantras of our day are "single-issue right wingers" and are therefore a literal SECURITY RISK to the well-being of the United States of America! This is simply amazingly incredible!

A free society that sits on its hands, remains silent and watches Orwell's *1984* unfold before its very eyes will surely not be free in the days and weeks ahead. We have chosen leaders in all three branches of our government who are hell-bent (perhaps literally) on completely restructuring the socio-political context of our country and culture. In a few short months, there will be millions of us who are not nearly as free as we thought our Constitution guaranteed because we have just been branded "Security Risks!"

This is the foolishness of "man's wisdom" run amuck and as we are told in the Proverbs—God literally laughs at such "wisdom!"

Chapter 4

CHANGE!

"I'm starting with the man in the mirror…
If you wanna make the world a better place
Take a look at yourself, and then make a change."
MICHAEL JACKSON, "MAN IN THE MIRROR"

CAMPAIGN SLOGANS, POLITICAL speeches, pop music, and even government web pages: Everywhere we turned during the 2008 elections and beyond, we heard the echoes of monastic chants calling for change. Radio, television, Facebook, Twitter, MySpace, and even the antiquity of newsprint have all been inundated: "We are the ones we've been waiting for. We are the change that we seek." Change we can believe in. Change we need. Vote for Change. Change.gov. A Time for Change. Change in our Time… "If you wanna make the world a better place, take a look at yourself and…Change!"

However, is change always something to be celebrated, or are there times when proclamations of change should be received with caution and concern? The answer lies in another question: Change from what to what? What value, idea, agenda or behavior do you want to change; and is that change moving you from bad to good or good to bad? Does such change represent that which is decent and beautiful or that which is depraved and ugly?

You see, change is a concept that cannot stand alone. Change needs to be supported by definition.

You see, change is a concept that cannot stand alone. Change needs to be supported by definition. Change means very little until we know what we intend to embrace and what we intend to discard. Change is akin to an empty glass that must be filled before it has any moral value or ethical weight. The container is not what matters but rather what you put in it. A glass can be filled with water or vinegar or with poison. "Change," likewise, can be filled full of that which is nourishing, that which is bitter or that which is deadly. The lessons of history (from Stalin to Pol Pot or Jefferson to King or even from the Jackson Five to Michael Jackson) show us time and again that until we know what it is that we are changing, why we are changing it and where such change will take us; we drink of the cup of "change" either to our advancement or our own demise.

So yes: Let's "take a look at ourselves." Let's "start with the man in the mirror." What do you see?

At first glance, you may be pleased to see the eyes of Michael Jackson staring back at you. These are good eyes. They are kind eyes. You see eyes that cry for a "better world" and a "better place." These are eyes that beg for justice, freedom, love, and mercy. You want to feed the hungry, help the poor, care for the environment, move beyond racial stereo-types, and abolish hatred and prejudice. You want to make a change. You want to eliminate all that is bad in our world and restore all that is good. You hunger and thirst for righteous-ness, and you disdain all that is unjust and unfair. You despise hypocrisy and you defend integrity. What you see in the man in the mirror is a savior and saint. "We are the world! We are the people! We are the ones to make a brighter day, so let's start giving! We are the "change we have been waiting for." We are the solution. We are good and we are right!

But stop before you walk away from this mirror with such confidence and self-assurance. Perhaps we need to look a bit closer before we turn away. As we gaze a bit deeper into the eyes of Michael, we see eyes staring back that are not as clear as we thought. In fact, these pupils are shadowy and opaque for they are disguised and hidden behind dark glasses.

This second glance in the mirror becomes increasingly unsettling, doesn't it? We are now making eye contact with a man who is tragically trapped and confused. Embarrassed eyes tell us of one who is ashamed of his duplicity and humiliated by his own hypocrisy. These are sad and self-conscious eyes.

Staring back at us, we see a man calling for change in racial relations who was ironically willing to change his racial iden-tity by changing the color of his skin. We see a man apparently so uncomfortable with his own appearance that he invited plastic surgeons to change what was natural and beautiful into something contrived, plastic and grotesque.

We see a man whose lyrics champion the innocence of chil-dren but yet stood accused of using children for anything but innocent ends.

As we look into this mirror one last time, we see a man staring back at us who was pleading with the people of the world to grow up, to mature, to stop acting like spoiled, selfish children and to "change" into adults. But this is the same man who served as the poster-child for post-modernity's youth-obsessed culture, and its consequent disdain for chronological maturity. A Peter Pan, Michael at 50 years of age stubbornly denied the inevitable and refused to acknowledge the "change" of growing older, of living in the reality of adulthood, and instead lived in the fantasy world of his own Neverland

Do you see it? Do you recognize the man in this mirror? Those eyes staring back at you are your own. It is your own culture. It is your own community. It is your own corporation. It is your church, your government, your school, your university. It is you. As Narcissus gazed with youthful arrogance at his own reflection and drowned in self-congratulatory infatuation, so we seem to be captivated by the grotesque monstrosity of our own making that we see in the mirror. We look through the dark glasses, clouded by our own constructs, our own opinions, our own agendas, our own animal instincts; and we call for change. We deceive ourselves in the seclusion of our own little Neverlands, and we seem to be oblivious to the fact that much of what we are changing makes us look all the more fake, disfigured and pathetic. We seem oblivious to the obvious that everyone else sees: Change, if it is defined by the created rather than the Creator, is a very ugly and self-destructive thing. We look absurd and we don't even know it.

Change means very little until we know what we intend to embrace and what we intend to discard.

The glass of change will be filled (no void is ever left empty). It will either be filled with wine that is enduring and pure, or it will be filled with the toxic tonic of self. The elixir of narcissism leads to an early death for all who drink of it. If "we are the change we have been waiting for and if we are the change that we seek," if we are the ones, if we are the people, if it's all about us; then we should all rightly fear that we may indeed be drinking of this cup with poison dripping from the smirk of our self-confident lips.

Chapter 5

PRIDE AND PREJUDICE: IT'S GOD-AWFUL!

A DUST-UP BETWEEN Senator Barbara Boxer and the head of the National Black Chamber of Commerce was the talk of the town during the summer of 2009. In case you missed it, here is a brief version of what took place.

On July 16, 2009, Barbara Boxer in her official capacity as the ranking senator from the State of California was conducting a Senate hearing on environmental policy. In keeping with the Senator's partisan biases, she attempted to stack the rhetorical deck in favor of the Obama administration's Goreistic Green assumptions and all concurrent social and economic goals. With this as the context, one expert called before Senator Boxer's committee was the president and CEO of the National Black Chamber of Commerce, Harry C. Alford. The following is a summary of the exchange in question.

Barbara Boxer began by quoting a resolution on climate change from the NAACP (Note: In case you missed the obvious here, Mr. Alford is African-American and Senator Boxer is Caucasian). The Senator attempted to use this document as a challenge to Mr. Alford's position. Mr. Alford took umbrage and tried to get Senator Boxer to clarify why she was referring to the NAACP document as her primary source of rebuttal when the NAACP was essentially expressing a generic concern for the environment rather than a cart blanche endorsement of cap and trade policies. Feeling frustrated (and perhaps a bit cornered) Senator Boxer brought an additional source to bear from another African-American named John Grant who reportedly represents an organization called 100 Black Men of Atlanta. The dialogue and debate then proceeded as follows.

Alford: "Madam Chair that is condescending to me. I'm the CEO of the National Black Chamber of Commerce, and you're trying to put some other black group up to pit against me."

Boxer: "If this gentleman [referring, we can assume, to Mr. Grant] were here, he would be proud that he was being quoted."

Alford: "He should have been invited!"

Boxer: "...just so you know, he would be proud [second time she uses the word] that you are here... He's proud [third time she uses the word], I'm sure, that I am quoting him..."

Alford: "It is condescending to me...All that's condescending and I don't like it. It's racial. I don't like it. I take offense to it. As an African-American and a veteran of this country, I take offense to that. We are referring to the experts regardless of their color. And for someone to tell me, an African-American, college-educated veteran of the United States Army that I must contend with some other black group and put aside everything else in here—this has nothing to do with the NAACP and really has nothing to do with the National Black Chamber of Commerce. We're talking energy and that road the Chair went down, I think, is god-awful."

In the midst of the media flurry of conservative indignation and liberal angst that swirled around this political thrust and parry, may I suggest that we have perhaps missed the forest for the trees in our evaluation of the Senator's overtures and Mr. Alford's response?

The trees that we see are obvious: A conservative, black businessman finally has had enough, and he has the intestinal fortitude to say so. He rises up and shouts what millions are thinking: "Stop patting us on the head and telling us that you are proud of us! Stop implying that just because we are intelligent enough to express a coherent opinion that we should be proud of ourselves and proud of each other. And please—please stop pitting 'us black folk' against each other as a means of perpetuating your myopic partisan views. Black people have brains too! We are fully capable of self-confidence and self-direction. We don't have to agree with everything a white progressive says; and, frankly, we are sick of your patronizing condescension—especially in the face of your transparent efforts to 'keep us in line.' Your demagoguery, and its implicit racism is obvious and we don't like it!"

Yes, the soft pines of the Left's fallacious tolerance of everything but what it deems to be intolerable are waving their shadowy branches all around us aren't they?

When flustered we become more honest.

But look further beyond these trees, beyond the trunks and shrubs of agreement or disagreement with Alford or Boxer and look, as the Oxford Don C.S. Lewis admonishes us, "farther up and farther in." Step back and take a look at the forest.

Pride leads to every other vice. Pride is the complete anti-God state of mind.

Three times in her harangue of Alford, Senator Boxer used a derivative of the word "pride." Three times she said "he would be proud" or implied that "you should be proud." Three times she did what almost all of us do when flustered: She showed her cards and her real priorities. When cornered, we all do this. When we are set back on our heels by a counterpunch, we all, whether intentional or not, put up our strongest defense—our highest good—our summum bonum—our guiding apologetic—our fallback position, if you will. Watch any debate or argument. When it escalates beyond the point of the controlled and the scripted to the level of reflex, instinct and emotion; you will always find the underlying assumptions and values of the protagonist and antagonist. When flustered we become more honest. You do. I do. Alford did and so did Senator Boxer.

For Senator Boxer, the strongest counterpunch she could muster in the face of Mr. Alford's foray was that of pride. She repeated it three times. Proud! Proud! Proud! And therein we start to see the "forest" of her argument. Pride is the ultimate value. Pride is the trump card against all other hands. Boxer seems to almost be subconsciously paraphrasing Michael Douglas' infamous 1987 Wall Street quote whereby Gordon Gekko elevated another of the seven deadly sins (i.e., greed) to that of virtue versus vice. Can you hear her? "The point is ladies and gentlemen, that [pride], for lack of a better word, is good, [pride] is right, [pride] works. [Pride] clarifies, cuts through and captures the essence of the evolutionary spirit. [Pride] in all of its forms...has marked the upward surge of mankind...and [Pride], you mark my words will ... not only save [our environment and our economy] but [also] the...United States of America."

Once commenting on the infinite varieties of human waywardness, Chaucer said, "The root of all these seven [deadly] sins is Pride: the general root of all harms." Augustine added that Pride "inordinately enamored with its own power...despises the more just dominion of a higher authority." One of our most endearing twentieth century apologists, C.S. Lewis, ties it all together: "Pride leads to every other vice. Pride is the complete anti-God state of mind. Pride ultimately leads all who embrace it to declare: 'I admit. I am the universe. I am your God'" (*Perelandra*, C.S. Lewis 1965).

You see, Barbara Boxer's juvenile mantra of Pride...Pride... Pride, betrays a dark forest of rotting trees waving gnarly branches of arrogance, condescension, haughtiness, hubris, self-congratulation and the ultimate of all progressive self-refuting claims. It uncovers a sanctimonious call for tolerance while not tolerating anyone (especially a conservative, African-American business-

This kind of pride is indeed god-awful!

man) who dares to disagree and refuses to follow blindly and obediently behind the emperor of the Left who happens to be wearing no clothes.

Mr. Alford said it well. This kind of pride is indeed god-awful! It's awful in the eyes of God and awful as well to all who seek God and wish to be protected from the pride and prejudice of those among us who yearn to be God.

Chapter 6

A TEACHABLE MOMENT: SUMMIT OR SUMMONS?

IN ALL THE media hype and hoopla over the infamous July 2009 "Beer Summit" on the White House Rose Garden patio, something was conspicuously missing. The glaring omission: The event's purpose as expressed by the person who called the meeting to order in the first place.

You see, nearly every other Presidential "summit" in political memory has been preceded by months of negotiation whereby the vested parties haggled over and ultimately agreed upon the meeting's specific goals, objectives, and intended outcomes. Rules for dialogue were set in advance. The topics to be discussed were clarified. Expectations were well defined. The location for the event was determined. Furniture was selected, flags were positioned, and fanfare was controlled. All this was and is done in an effort to assure neutral footing for all involved; because everyone knows that without such clarity the meeting could easily gravitate toward the self-serving instincts of one party or the other; and that's not the purpose of a summit—is it??

But with the much ballyhooed "Beer Summit," such shared ownership of goals, strategy, and objectives seemed to be lacking. All we knew of the event's intended outcomes was what we were told by its One and only organizer and its One and only host. As far as we knew, no other input was offered (or sought?) and, in fact, it seemed to be clear that our President was not seeking mutual consent on the target that he obviously had in his sights. Mr. Obama knew what he was after: The only reason for the meeting, we were told by the One who called it, was that it would be a "teachable moment."

Teachable moment? I don't know about you, but when I hear these words used by someone in authority, they almost always mean that this is a moment for the person in authority to teach, and you and me to learn. In other words, the person calling the "teachable moment" to order is saying, "I am going to talk and you need to listen. It is a time for the teacher to teach and the student to learn."

So what I argue has been missing in the media coverage of this entire "summit" is the presumed pedagogical paradigm of our Teacher-In-Chief. To say it another way—shouldn't we be asking what exactly it was that the president felt needed to be taught and to whom was he directing his teaching?

For example, did our president teach Dr. Gates that he should be thankful to the police for putting their lives on the line in responding so quickly to a potential robbery of the Harvard professor's own residence?

Did our president instruct Dr. Gates that he should be grateful for neighbors who cared enough about the collective safety of the community (and the professor's property) to make the 911 call in the first place?

Did our president lecture Dr. Gates that he should be thankful for a police officer who was not so naïve as to accept, at first blush, the professor's flippant explanations that "this is my house" and instead asked for identification from the very one who was attempting forcible entry into that same house?

Did the president edify everyone at this "summit" that it is unwise and presumptuous to take sides in a disagreement and label one person "stupid" before you even know the details and facts of the matter in dispute?

Did Mr. Obama's lesson plan include anything about the time-tested truth of justice being blind and the implicit racism of assuming mistreatment and victimization simply because of what you see in the skin color of your accuser?

And finally, did the president ever confront the professor and teach him that rude and angry vitriol almost always betrays the self-righteousness of one's ego rather than the objective rightness of one's arguments?

Yes, this was a teachable moment, but somehow I doubt that the above pedagogy (i.e. method of teaching) was ever employed; and I sincerely question whether our president's lesson plan included any of the ideas thus described.

My suspicion: This was not so much a *summit* to debate ideas and differing opinions but, rather, it was more of a *summons* where the One in charge, *taught* others what to think, what to do, and what to say. Because, after all, to disagree with the principal when you are summoned into his office for a "teachable moment" would be—well how should I say it—stupid.

Chapter 7

ARE FISH REAL?

GET READY FOR some twists and turns. This one will keep you on your toes.

Not long after the bombings of September 2001, a forum was held at George Washington University. The two guest speakers were Drs. David Horowitz and Ward Churchill. Horowitz, a former intellectual leader of the radical-left, previously served the likes of the Black Panthers and similar organizations but is now an outspoken "convert." He is a conservative. Ward Churchill, on the other hand, is the infamous professor from the University of Colorado who made headlines because of his bold claim that Americans deserved the terrorism of 9/11 because of our complicity with the evils of western capitalism.

The topic discussed at this forum was "Politics in the Classroom." The organizers of the event sought to encourage an open exchange of perspectives and to ponder the pros and cons of Churchill's views versus those of Horowitz. As is true of any debate, the goal was for the students to listen, be educated, and then decide who had the better ideas.

But, in the midst of this debate Dr. Churchill changed the rules. In his opening comments he declared: "There is no truth." He then proceeded to lecture all those present on how all truth claims were merely dominant orthodoxies imposed upon cultures and societies by those in power. In this assertion Churchill nullified any goal of finding the better ideas or the right answers. In one sweeping generalization, he claimed that education isn't about the pursuit of truth; it's about the construction of personal narratives and nuanced opinions. If you are looking for rational conclusions grounded in objective facts, then you are in the wrong place.

Now some of you may agree with Churchill. You may be saying, "Who are you to imply that there is such a thing as a good or bad culture or a right or a wrong religion, or that there is a superior or inferior view of art, music or literature?" You may go further and ask, "Who are you to claim that some political and economic systems are better than others?" And you may maintain, "There is no such thing as objective truth, because an enlightened and open-minded society knows every-thing is relative."

If you are tempted to take this position, you are not alone. To the contrary, you are in the note-worthy company of not only Ward Churchill but countless others in the contemporary university who claim that they are absolutely sure that there are no absolutes. They suggest that everyone knows that nothing can be known. They are confident in their criticism of those who are confident. They just can't tolerate those who are intolerant, and they simply hate those people who are hateful. With what appears to be unthinking unanimity, these hordes of free-thinking professors parrot this Churchillian party-line and declare with bold confidence and in the face of little opposition: "There is no such thing as truth, and that's the truth." When you ask them if they are sure, they say, "Yes, we are sure that nothing is sure."

Okay, I'll stop. Forgive me. Even though these oxymoronic mental gymnastics are so much fun, I won't subject you to my sadistic pleasure any longer.

An educated person is one who knows how to distinguish between faulty logic and its errors, as well as sound reasoning and its correctness.

My point is this. How in the world can a university organize a debate, which by definition aims to advance two opposing positions and their corresponding claims of proof and veracity, and then allege (with a straight face) to believe all views are equal and no idea is any better or worse than another? Even more, how can a professor who asserts that Americans deserve to be killed for their evil ways, claim that there is no such thing as truth upon which to judge America's behavior as being evil? How can this same professor say he knows he is right and his opponent is wrong when his own declared epistemology (i.e., his foundation for knowing) presupposes that he himself can't know anything? Finally, if you agree with Churchill, on what basis do you agree with him and disagree with me?

One way to answer these questions is to go back to the purpose of education. I will show my cards here. I believe that a good university trains its students to wrestle with the multiple ideas of our world with the goal of discarding the fallacious and embracing the effectual. An educated person, if he or she is nothing else, is one who knows how to distinguish between faulty logic and its errors, as well as sound reasoning and its correctness. When it comes down to it, education is in the business of giving us the means of measuring the rightness and/or wrongness of all ideas so that we will, thus, have the ability to move toward the freedom that is born of truth and away from the slavery sired by lies.

In challenging the intellectual elitists of our day, Louis Bromfield in *The Triumph of the Egghead,* talks about people of "spurious and intellectual pretensions...so given to examining all sides of a question that [they] become quite addled while remaining always in the same spot." Gerard Reed (in *C.S. Lewis Explores Vice and Virtue*) challenges us further. He critiques those aligned with Churchill and his ilk by saying: "Amazingly, in today's colleges and universities, many students parrot skeptical professors and declare, after four years of study, that all they've learned is that they know nothing ...They seem to think their minds are like loosely woven fishing nets that move through the water without catching any fish."

> *As the goal of fishing is to actually catch fish, so the goal of education is to actually find the truth.*

In these simple words, Reed reminds us of the obvious: Dr. Churchill, the fish are real. There is, indeed, something in the water. As the goal of fishing is to actually catch fish, so the goal of education is to actually find the truth.

Chapter 8

THIS MEDICINE
MAKES ME SICK

I LEARNED AN axiom years ago from a mentor of mine, Dr. David McKenna, who served as president of Spring Arbor College, my alma mater. In 1980, he was one of two individuals on the short list for Secretary of Education under the newly-elected president of the United States, Ronald Reagan.

Dr. McKenna is perhaps one of the most gifted orators I have ever known. His mastery of the podium rivaled that of the Great Communicator who nearly chose him to be a member of his Cabinet. He is one of those rare leaders who has clearly been blessed by God with both the Midas touch and a golden tongue.

Here is a tidbit of Dr. McKenna's wisdom that I will never forget: "The best predictor of future behavior is past behavior."

Pretty simple and straight forward isn't it? Not a lot of fluff or verbosity. In a short sentence of nine words, we are reminded to consider the obvious: If you want to know what is going to happen in the future, it is best to look at the past behavior of the people in question. What they did in the past, is likely to be exactly what they will do in the future.

We have taught teenagers that the concept of sin is irrelevant.

With this as context, I suggest that we sift the idea of a "public option" for healthcare through the grid of Dr. McKenna's wisdom. In other words, let's look at the past and ask ourselves an obvious question: Are there any examples of "public options" that might be predictive models for what we can expect—good and bad—from another government-run program?

Let's look at the "public option" of State-run education for example.

The good news is that access has increased, and essentially anyone who wants to go to school or college can. The bad news is that the schools and colleges these people now attend are mediocre at best.

The idea of public-funded/government-controlled schools is in many ways a complete and unmitigated failure. Look around at the consequences of this idea and the havoc it has wreaked on our health, fortune, happiness and freedom for the past 50 or 60 years. Many students can't read or write or perform the most elementary of mathematical tasks, but they graduate anyway. Many teachers can't teach but they receive tenure anyway. Standardized tests have been "recalibrated" (i.e. dumbed down) because of decades of declining scores. Grade inflation makes a student's GPA essentially meaningless in assessing his/her potential for collegiate success. Because of ACLU threats, the good teachers that do try to minister within this mess are required to perpetuate a "morally neutral" curriculum. Essentially these same teachers watch helplessly on the sidelines as some students go about the grizzly business of raping and killing each other. Columbine and Virginia Tech at times seem to be more the norm on the nightly news than an aberration.

At the behest of government-run education, we have taught teenagers that the concept of sin is irrelevant. Then we wonder why our sixteen-year-old girls show up for their sophomore year pregnant and proud of it. Colleges have handed out condoms from coast to coast while failing to share with these young people the Department of Health and Human Services data that warns of an epidemic of STDs. Public education has touted the merits of the "liberal" arts—a robust and open exchange of ideas as the ideal—while our elected public servants boldly burn the flag of academic freedom declaring that they "won't tolerate the intolerant."

So, here is the question: If the best predictor of future behavior is past behavior, why would we think that government-run hospitals will be any different than government-run education? If the State-supported classroom is a screwed up mess lacking any sense of moral clarity, and if the same classroom refuses to accommodate our unalienable rights of religious liberty and freedom of speech, then why should we expect anything different would prevail in a government-funded hospital room?

Let me put it another way: If you can't speak of God at the curbside of your local schoolhouse, then what makes you think that you will be able to sing a hymn to God at someone's bedside in your local public-house-of-healthcare? Moreover, why would a doctor be permitted to talk about Christ's forgiveness with dying patients in the public hospital, when that same doctor is prohibited from talking about Christ's birth with healthy students in the public high school? Or how about this more timely example: If a priest can't speak of God as the giver of human rights in Ted Kennedy's local public school then why would you think the same priest would be permitted to administer last rights to Ted Kennedy at his local public hospital?

If the best predictor of future behavior is past behavior, why would we think that government-run hospitals will be any different than government-run education?

If it is funded by the State, then it has to be totally secular—right??

The best predictor of future behavior is past behavior. If we want to know where government-funded healthcare will lead, then all we have to do is to look down the path already trod by government-funded education.

Ideas have consequences and the ideas being debated right now are not new. They have been in play for years, and we, therefore, have a clear predictor of what lies ahead. Unfortunately the medicine we are about to take has not made us well in the past, but to the contrary, it seems to have made us sick—perhaps even sick unto death.

Chapter 9

WORLDVIEWS HAVE CONSEQUENCES

HOW DO WE KNOW which arguments are right and which are wrong? How can we distinguish between claims that are accurate and those that are mistaken? How do we determine what is true and what is false?

Before we go any further, let me say this: Congratulations if you even care. For in a post-modern culture where over 60 percent of Americans say they don't believe in any absolute standards of right and wrong and that all "truth claims" and all moral judgments are relative, it is encouraging to find a remnant wishing to pursue truth rather than construct it. I think you should be applauded if you are eager to debate the veracity of certain ideas. You are already halfway home while others haven't yet even begun the journey.

But I digress. Let's get back to the question. How do you assess arguments for truth?

To set the context for an answer, we should first acknowledge the negative. There are certain methods of debate that we should beware of because they often lead down the wrong path—to darkness rather than light—to dishonesty rather than candor.

First, beware of arguments that shoot the messenger and, thus, obfuscate—confuse or confound—the message. This is an age-old fallacy of diversion that goes back to the days of Socrates. It is technically called the *argumentum ad hominem*—which means an "argument addressed to the person" instead of the issue. In other words, you attack the antagonist rather than address his or her ideas. When you see someone attempting to brand liberals as "loons" or conservatives as "fundies," it is a dead giveaway. When a politician calls those who disagree with him "ignorant," or when a professor labels opponents as "fools," you know the argument is more about political agendas, personal attacks, and protecting opinions than about rational debate. Beware of these tactics. They rarely lead you to your goal of deciphering fact from fiction.

Another tactic to beware of is that of assumption. When a person says something is true, you can't assume it is so. This is a non sequitur—which means that the conclusion doesn't logically follow from the argument. It is perhaps the most common of all fallacies, so common we often fall prey to it unknowingly. A pastor makes a claim so we accept it as fact. A parent sets a rule so we take it as the final word. A professor denies something so we assume he is telling the truth.

But our experience has shown us time and again that trusting personal claims is not a good measure of truth.

In order to trust, we must first verify.

Hitler told Chamberlain that he wouldn't invade Eastern

Europe. Nixon denied complicity in Watergate. Clinton said he "didn't have sex with that woman." Ward Churchill claimed he didn't plagiarize, and Eric Pianka (despite the testimony of multiple students, colleagues, interviews, and audio recordings) now denies he has called for forced sterilization and the massive depopulation of the human race. Simply saying something doesn't make it so. History has taught us that truth must be grounded in something more stable than mankind's proven propensity for deception. Haven't we learned that in order to trust, we must first verify?

So how do we do this? In the midst of conflicting statements, how do we verify what is true and refute what is false? How can we have confidence in what is really honest and trustworthy?

History has taught us that truth must be grounded in something more stable than mankind's proven propensity for deception.

Perhaps the answer lies in paradigms and not people—in guiding ideologies rather than fallible men and women. Here is a question: Are we missing the forest for the trees when we listen to ad hominem attacks and non sequitur arguments; arguments that presuppose name-calling; arguments that assume a statement is true just "because I said so?" Do we get distracted by fallacies and miss seeing the facts?

In our pursuit of truth, we must look past the distractions of people and instead look to the power of ideas. The specific ideas associated with a given worldview set the context for us to assess the truthfulness of that worldview's proponents. Marxism set the stage for Stalin's deception. Nazism was the predicate for Hitler's military subterfuge. The ideological consequences of Darwinism as espoused by everyone from Carl Sagan to Eric Pianka are, likewise, unavoidable. If men and women are of no greater intrinsic value than other forms of biological matter, then there is no reason to argue for our existence versus that of a lizard or a virus. If survival of the fittest is the optimal value, then morality has no meaning and humanity's belief in truth is merely unscientific self-deception, and "un-Darwinian" (as declared by Richard Rorty, himself a noted Darwinist).

A politician calls those who disagree with him, "ignorant," or when a professor labels opponents as "fools," you know the argument is more about political agendas, personal attacks, and protecting opinions than about rational debate.

Ideas have consequences. Some worldviews admit that truth exists and that we are obligated to pursue it and speak it. Other worldviews boldly state that there is no such thing as truth; that a religious moral compass is the opiate of the masses; and that "survival of the fittest" is the only built-in, ruling law of nature and of man. All other "laws" are merely the sum total of one organism jockeying for power over another.

If your goal is to find what is true, you might just be better off looking at ideas first—before you listen to people. Perhaps guiding worldviews and their proven consequences are the best starting point for assessing sincerity and answering the question "What is the truth?"

Chapter 10

DUALISM, MULTIPLICITY, RELATIVISM... AND FRANKIE

I HAVE SPENT MUCH of my professional life in the halls of universities, studying at the knee of scholars who embrace human development theory as if it is our salvation. I, frankly, could bore all of you to tears by talking about this stuff.

Wouldn't it be fun to have breakfast and chat about the sequential nature of Chickering's seven vectors? Or we could enjoy a cup of coffee as we debate Kohlberg's three stages of moral development. In the midst of this excitement, I am sure you would want to stick around for dinner and ponder Perry's four schemes of dualism, multiplicity, relativism, and commitment in relativism. These are phases of life where we all move from a childhood of dualistic absolutes to an adolescence of multiplicity where we reject the simplistic notions of right or wrong, then on to an early adulthood of relativism where we embrace the pragmatic good of "personal values," and finally to full maturity where we settle-in and "commit" ourselves to the goodness of a specific lifestyle—relative though it may be.

Oh, but we shouldn't stop here. We would need to conclude our conversation with the Holy Grail of human development theory: The Plus-One Concept. This shibboleth tells us that all growth is incremental. Moral development is realized in sequential steps rather than broad leaps. To misdiagnose the "starting point" is to miss the whole point. As educators we must assume that all students are dualistic, black and white thinkers. If we are to honor the "plus-one concept," our goal must be to first assess the present developmental stage of the pupil and then to challenge these students to abandon their childlike affection for absolutes and move up one rung on the developmental ladder and, thus, embrace multiplicity as the next natural phase of life.

If I haven't lost you already, don't panic. I won't subject you to this torture any further but for one exception: I would like to point out the bankruptcy and dangerous consequences of these ideas.

Let me tell you a story about a class I taught a few years back and of a student named Frankie. Prior to moving to Oklahoma, I served as the dean of students at a liberal arts college in Michigan. In my role as dean, I also taught a class or two. One of these classes was the standard and obligatory freshman orientation course. Each year, I sought to "orient" my new students to life at a liberal arts institution and to challenge them to wrestle with what it meant to be a disciplined thinker. In this context, I had a traditional assignment. I required my students to watch the movie, *Schindler's List,* and then to write a standard, three-page paper. My intent was to force the students to think about the "Christian culture" of WWII Germany and then to ask themselves these questions:

- Why would any group of people ever succumb to the atrocities of the Holocaust?

- Why did the German culture—the culture out of which the Protestant Reformation came—lose sight of the truth to the extent that they could no longer recognize something like genocide and mass murder as being so clearly evil and wrong?

Amazingly, in today's colleges and universities, many students parrot skeptical professors and declare, after four years of study, that all they've learned is that they know nothing

After watching this movie, one of my students turned in a paper that was fairly well written. Frankie had obviously paid attention and was engaged with the film. Her report of the movie was quite thorough, but it was the concluding sentence that I will never forget. Incredible as it seems, after watching this heart-wrenching movie and summarizing its plot, historical accuracy, and detail, Frankie critiqued the moral decisions surrounding the holocaust by saying: "Who am I to judge the Germans?" She could not bring herself to tell me that the Holocaust was wrong!

For years, I, along with most all of my peers in higher education, assumed that the human development theory was simply and purely an empirical fact. We believed that students came to college with dualistic and foreclosed minds where everything was black and white, right or wrong. We claimed that these students came to us with authority as the basis of all moral judgment. If the pastor said it was true, it was true. If Mom said it was right, it was right. If Dad said it was wrong, it was wrong. Accordingly, we in the ivory tower believed it was our obligation to challenge these students to grow beyond the dualism of a Judeo-Christian ethic, take off the blinders, and embrace the multiple and various facets of "truth." Surely our young people needed to step away from the comforts of home and church and become more nuanced and "mature" in their morality and in their thinking.

Most young people today do not have the intellectual training and moral confidence to defend the logic of immutable moral standards.

I no longer believe this. In his book *Educating Post-Modern America, Generation X Goes to College,* Peter Sax contends that one of the basic characteristics of today's college students (and perhaps culture as a whole) is the pervasive and oxymoronic belief in absolute relativism. Sax argues that opinions are all that matter in the classrooms, boardrooms and bedrooms of contemporary life. It isn't that everything is black and white, right or wrong, but to the contrary, today nothing is black or white and nothing is right or wrong. Dualism is no longer the starting point. To the contrary, personal opinion rather than objective standards has become the final measure of all truth. The relative value of any action or belief is the only basis for judgment. Like Frankie so poignantly reminds us, one value or another is simply a matter of personal choice and personal preference. It's all relative— who are we to judge the Germans?

Is my story of Frankie an aberration? Is Peter Sax referring to young people other than those in our schools, our churches, and our neighborhoods? Is this a critique of a culture elsewhere—somebody else's but not ours?

All I know is this: Frankie taught me a lesson. She awakened me to the sobering limitations of prevailing academic fads. Human development theory has its place, but it falls far short of providing the "liberal" environment and consequent learning that it claims as its highest good.

You see, the word "liberal" implies liberation. And implicit in the word "liberation" is the presupposition that there are bad things from which we should be liberated. These things are not bad because we think so. They are bad simply because they

Ideas matter.

Ideas have

consequences.

are. The Holocaust was evil not just in the minds of those who disagreed with it. It was explicitly and absolutely bad, because it violated an immutable and transcendent moral standard. It was, is, and always will be simply wrong to incinerate people in furnaces because you have more political power than they do.

But here is the sobering reality—our young people today (and I have had tons of them under my tutelage) do not have the intellectual training and moral confidence to defend the logic of the previous several sentences.

Ideas matter. Ideas that disparage the time-tested truths of an earlier day while fawning over the newest intellectual fads may lead us down a very dangerous path. Maybe dualism isn't all that bad after all.

Chapter 11

DORM BROTHELS

"That is what happens to those who pluck and eat fruits at the wrong time and in the wrong way...The fruit is good, but they loathe it ever after. All get what they want; they do not always like it."

ASLAN IN C.S. LEWIS' *THE MAGICIAN'S NEPHEW*

IN THE *CHRONICLES OF NARNIA,* C.S. Lewis tells the story of the young boy named Digory who is sent on a journey by Aslan to retrieve an apple from a particular garden beyond the western mountains. The reason given to the boy for his trial is that the great Lion desired to plant a tree that will protect His kingdom from evil for generations to come. The boy is not to eat the apple in question. He is simply to pluck it from its branch, place it in his breast pocket and return it to Aslan, unblemished.

Upon making the trek, riding atop the winged horse, Fledge, Digory arrives at his destination. It is a walled garden protected by a great golden gate with a silver inscription that paradoxically warns that fruit intended for others should never be stolen for oneself: "For those who steal or those who climb my wall shall find their heart's desire and find despair."

Entering through the gate, Digory obeys Aslan's instructions. Tempted though he is by the delicious smell of the fruit, he decides he must do as he is told. He overcomes his desire and instead secures the apple and turns to leave the garden.

But as he does so, the boy is confronted by an evil witch. Her knowing smile betrays her. She has juice dripping from the corners of her mouth. "Don't you see fool," she says, "That one bite of the apple would give you your heart's desire?"

"All get what they want" but "they do not always like it."

Digory persists. He evades the witch and returns to Aslan. There at the Lion's knee he is reminded that there is an element of truth in the witch's seductions. Yes indeed, eating the apple would bring satisfaction. But to do so at the "wrong time and in the wrong way" would ultimately lead the boy to loathe, not love the object of his appetite. "All get what they want" but "they do not always like it," Aslan tells Digory.

I thought of this story recently while I was reading an essay titled *Dorm Brothels* by Vigen Guroian, professor of theology at Loyola College in Baltimore.

In his essay, Dr. Guroian laments the sexual dysfunction prevalent on his campus as well as that of most all other colleges and universities of our land. After sharing page after page of lurid detail of the incidents of sexual exploitation and sexual use and abuse rife within co-ed dorms [and all other living environments for that matter] at Loyola, Guroian references Aldous Huxley's *Brave New World* as a metaphor for today's campus. He contends that the loss of self-restraint and self-respect in the contemporary university is akin to the abolition of marriage, the end of courtship, and the loss of sexual intimacy described in *Brave New World*.

> *The loss of self-restraint and self-respect in the contemporary university is akin to the abolition of marriage, the end of courtship, and the loss of sexual intimacy.*

Guroian goes on to tell how a young Loyola co-ed agreed with the parallels he had drawn between Huxley and her campus: "Dr. Guroian," the student said, "It is more like *Brave New World* here than you think...Most [students] are not looking for a romantic relationship; they...see the new freedom and plethora of sexual opportunities and simply take what they can get. They get to college, and it's an amusement park with so many different enticing rides, one would be missing out on the whole experience to settle with the first one tried."

Dr. Guroian then cites this woman's conclusion: "Coed dormitories—are they an ideal situation or a sad form of prostitution? You go out with your friends on your terms. After a few drinks, you're both attracted. Interested and lonely, you go together, no obligations, no responsibilities, and no rules. Then there is that late-night 'booty call.' This has become such a custom of the college lifestyle [that] most have come to accept it, although maybe not respect it. If it were really the ideal situation, the walk home the next day wouldn't be called 'the walk of shame.'"

In *The Great Divorce,* C.S. Lewis contends that there are only two kinds of people in the end: Those who say to God, "Thy will be done;" and those to whom God says, "thy will be done."

Ideas matter.

Digory submitted to the grandest idea of all—something bigger than his own desires and stronger than his own passions. He declared to Aslan, "Thy will be done" and he, thus, tasted the fruit of the great Lion's grace and he "enjoyed it."

The college student in Dr. Guroian's *Dorm Brothels* (and by association, all of us who are complicit in this educational model) will bear the consequences of the power of ideas. Standing with juice dripping from the corner of one's mouth, it is possible to hear the words, "Thy will be done. You will get what you want. But beware; you will loathe it ever after. You will not always like it."

Chapter 12

FISH ON
THE BEACH

WE ALL LIKE to share our "war stories" from days gone by. I believe we enjoy doing this because our personal narratives are often mirrors that reflect our own questions and convictions, our priorities and discoveries. In this context, permit me to tell you a story stemming from my days as a dean of students.

A few years ago a student named Hans came into my office. He was frustrated and disappointed. Hans was one of our best. He was bright, articulate and thoughtful. He enjoyed the give and take of a good debate. He was quick on this feet, and, as a burgeoning sociologist, he was finding various political, organizational, and developmental theories to be valuable tools in critiquing people and evaluating their actions and attitudes.

During this visit to my office, Hans spent about an hour or so telling me quite eloquently what was wrong with the faculty, staff and students of our college. Hans had a solid grasp of the theories he was learning in the classroom. His ability to use these ideas as a guide in assessing the problems and failures of our specific campus was exceptional.

After listening for a while, I interrupted and said, "Hans, let me give you an assignment. I would like you to develop a theory of fish." I proceeded to tell Hans that I wanted him to take a pad of paper and a pencil and go down to the local lake and walk along the beach. While there, Hans was to document everything he saw. These observations would serve as the foundation for his theory of fish.

I went further and said, "Let's assume that as you walk along the beach you see fish lying about in the sand. They are crusty and gasping for air, their eyes are bulging out and they smell really bad. So you take out your pad and pencil and you write: Fish are caked with sand. They have eyes that bulge out. They gasp for air and have a pungent odor. Fish stink. Is your theory accurate?"

There is but one good: That is God. Everything else is good when it looks to Him and bad when it turns from Him.

Hans looked at me with confusion. After waiting a bit, I rescued him from having to answer and said, "Hans, yes, your theory is accurate. Your conclusions are empirically valid. You have a sound understanding that reflects exactly on what you could see, touch, taste and smell. But does your theory tell you all that you need to know and want to know about fish?" I went further. "Hans, your theory is based on objective research, but it is also based on the observation of a broken world. It fails to recognize one obvious thing. If you would pick these fish up and put them back in the water where they belong, they would flourish and be what they were intended to be."

Sometimes I wonder about our focus. Often, looking at people through the lens of our theories seems to be akin to looking at fish on the beach: accurate, yes—but incomplete. In assessing the world around us, we tend to be satisfied with political and personal theories that are merely "accurate" depictions of a fallen world. In seeing the dirty, dying, crusty, and confused nature of mankind, we conclude that this condition is optimal and indeed the way people are supposed to be. We see "fish on the beach" and we assume that this is what fish are. We may try to dust off the sand and shade them from the sun but we fail to see the obvious: The beach is not where they belong. We should put them in the water.

C.S. Lewis, in *The Great Divorce,* says, "Brass is mistaken for gold more easily than is clay...There is but one good: That is God. Everything else is good when it looks to Him and bad when it turns from Him." His point is this: Philosophers as diverse as Nietzshe to Neuhaus and Fromm to Frankl have all agreed that what makes us human is our search for meaning. We all are looking for the best things—the right things—the enduring things. We all look for answers and in the process we sometimes mistake brass for gold. We are too easily satisfied with the inferior. We confuse our "accurate" theories that represent the way things are, for the immutable Truths that represent the way things "ought" to be. We forget that a theory is good only when it turns toward *Shalom* (i.e., the immutable, unalienable and intended order) and always incomplete when it turns away.

> *We all look for answers and in the process we sometimes mistake brass for gold.*

Now let me be clear. As an educator I am passionate about ideas. Constructing theories and finding rational explanations is what I do. It is my obligation (and likewise yours) to understand the most current research and to use it for the benefit of our students and schools and for the good of our corporations and our culture. But we must not mistake this brass for what is truly gold. As C.S. Lewis says: "Only by looking beyond ourselves does the brass of theory become the gold of Truth." Only by looking through eyes bigger than personal constructs, popular fads, or political power can we see beyond a broken world and recognize that we must pick "the fish" up and throw them back into the "water" where they belong. Only then will people flourish and become what they were intended to be in the first place.

Chapter 13

ESCAPING THE UNDERWORLD

"When you try to think out clearly what this sun must be, you cannot tell me. You can only tell me it is like the lamp. Your sun is a dream and there is nothing in that dream that was not copied from the lamp. The lamp is the real thing; the sun is but a tale..."

THE EMERALD WITCH IN C.S. LEWIS' *THE SILVER CHAIR*

In *The Silver Chair,* the fifth book in the Chronicles of Narnia series, we find three main characters: two children named Scrubb and Jill and a Narnian friend called Puddleglum. These three adventurers meet up with Aslan who gives them instructions to venture into a dark underground world in search of Rilian, the Prince of Narnia, who has been kidnapped and held captive by none other than an evil witch.

Well, in the midst of their journey through the deep caves of the Underworld they find the Prince. He is in a dark and damp cavern, tied to a silver chair that has mysterious powers over him. He has been brainwashed to believe that the witch is his ally not his captor, that darkness is light and that his bondage is freedom.

Upon discovering Prince Rilian, the kids and Puddleglum decide to take action. They untie the Prince so that they can escape the confines of the cave before the witch returns. But, alas, they are too late. The witch comes back and catches them before they can flee the darkness of the Underworld and return to the warm sun-drenched lands of Narnia.

Standing before the witch in a cave, barely lit by smoldering smudge pots, Jill, Scrubb, and Puddleglum confront their captor. They demand that she let them return home. They want to see the sun and feel its warm rays. They want to run in the cool of the evening, bathe in moon beams, lie in the grass, and count the stars. They want to escape from the ugly world of the witch's making and return instead to Narnia. They want to experience what is right and true. They want to be free. They want to be with Aslan.

Now here is what is interesting. In confronting the Prince and his friends, the witch doesn't use physical force. She instead chooses to use the power of words and ideas. Here is how Lewis describes it.

> "What is this sun that you all speak of?" [said the Witch] "Do you mean anything by the word? ...Can you tell me what it's like? ..."
>
> "Please it your Grace," said the Prince. "You see that lamp. It is round and yellow and gives light to the whole room; and hangeth moreover from the roof. Now that thing which we call the sun is like the lamp, only far greater and brighter. It giveth light to the whole Overworld and hangeth in the sky."

*"Hangeth from what, my lord?" asked the witch and then,
while they were all still thinking how to answer her, she
added, with another of her soft, silver laughs, "You see?
When you try to think out clearly what this sun must be, you
cannot tell me. You can only tell me it is like the lamp. Your
sun is a dream and there is nothing in that dream that was
not copied from the lamp. The lamp is the real thing; the sun
is but a tale, a children's story."*

Does this argument sound familiar?

In over twenty years of working within academia, I have
found today's campuses to be in many ways as dark and fake
as the witch's Underworld. The materialist says there is no truth beyond
what you can touch, feel, taste, and
see. As Carl Sagan declares, The
Cosmos is all there ever was and ever
will be. The post-modernist says there
is no truth at all. Foucault, Rorty,
Lyotard, and a host of others all join
with the Emerald Witch to declare
there are no suns, only lamps. Dreams
of Lions are merely "Religion's"

> *The materialist
> says there is no
> truth beyond
> what you can
> touch, feel,
> taste, and see.*

wishful hopes of what cats could be. There are no immutable
standards. There really is no such thing as good and evil—no
universal truths—no Narnia—no Overworld—no sky—no
sun—no Aslan. "You have seen lamps, and so you imagined a
bigger and better lamp and called it the sun. You've seen cats,
and now you want a bigger and better cat, and it's to be called
a Lion."

But there is a way out of this dark cave. Freedom is found
in the path of Puddleglum.

You see, in the midst of the witch's lies and manipulation (while the Prince and the children had given up and were mindlessly repeating the witch's mantra) Puddleglum decided to fight back. And this is how he did it. He got as close to what he knew to be real as he possibly could. He stepped in the fire: "While the Prince and the two children were standing with their heads hung down, their cheeks flushed, their eyes half closed, the strength all gone from them; the [witch's] enchantment almost complete...Puddleglum, desperately gathering all his strength, walked over to the fire...[and] with his bare foot he stamped on [it]... The pain itself made Puddleglum's head for a moment perfectly clear and he knew exactly what he really thought. There is nothing like a good shock of pain for dissolving certain kinds of magic."

Liberation can only happen when we have the courage to pursue reality.

The way to distinguish between what is false and what is fact is to follow Puddleglum. We must recognize that there are some things that are real and hot and true. To know the difference between "suns and lamps" and "lions and cats" we must get as close to reality as we possibly can. Stepping into the "fire" might hurt, but "there is nothing like a good shock of pain for dissolving certain kinds of magic."

Maybe liberation from the darkness of the cave can only happen when we have the courage to pursue reality—to step right into it—and not be satisfied with the chants and mantras of the witches of post-modernity.

Chapter 14

DO YOU REALLY WANT AN ANSWER?

OVER SIXTY YEARS AGO, in *The Abolition of Man*, C.S. Lewis challenged Christian scholars to enter the "town square" and the "market place of ideas." He argued that in failing to do so, we would become a society of men without chests; a culture of heartless people satisfied with our own subjective constructs and divorced from any common agreement of what is right and wrong; a culture of disconnected individuals who care little for what is immutable and enduring, accurate or true. The prophetic voice of the Oxford Don warned of a time when questions would lie fallow in a field of disingenuous inquiry with little interest in a harvest of answers.

Today indeed is a time of big questions—questions about things such as:

Life: When does it begin and when does it end and who has the right to define it and take it?

Global warming: Is its premise scientific, political, principled or pragmatic?

Today indeed is a time of big questions.

Sexuality: What is healthy and best for body, soul, family and society?

Tolerance: Are all worldviews and religions epistemologically and ontologically equal?

Justice: If Darwin's presupposition of "survival of the fittest" is canonized, then isn't the concept of justice rather arbitrary and meaningless? The strong should subdue the weak, shouldn't they? Let the evolutionary circle of life prevail. There is no moral reason for us object to those with power prevailing over those without it. In fact, isn't it true that "morality" is really nothing more than the subjective imposition of bourgeois rules upon their powerless victims?

Questions, questions, such important questions…but do we really want answers? Do we assume the existence of right and wrong, accuracy and inaccuracy in our asking, or do we care more about silencing our opponents than correcting our opinions? Do we want to learn or do we hope to lecture? Bottom line: Are we willing to work hard enough to find an answer even at the possibility of being wrong, or are we too easily satisfied and, thus, resting easily in our own personal ideologies or political agendas?

In *The Great Divorce,* Lewis challenges such intellectual laziness and political expediency. "Our opinions were not honestly come by," he said. "We simply found ourselves in contact with a certain current of ideas and plunged into it because it seemed modern and successful…You know, we just started automatically writing the kind of essays that got good marks and saying the kind of things that won applause."

He goes on: "You and I were playing with loaded dice. We didn't want the other to be true. We were afraid...afraid of a breach with the spirit of the age, afraid of ridicule..."

"Having allowed [ourselves] to drift, unresisting...accepting every half-conscious solicitation from our desires, we reached a point where we no longer believed [the Truth]. Just in the same way, a jealous man, drifting and unresisting, reaches a point at which he believes lies about his best friend."

Lewis concludes: "Once you were a child. Once you knew what inquiry was for. There was a time when you asked questions because you wanted answers, and were glad when you had found them. Become that child again...You have gone far wrong. Thirst was made for water; inquiry for truth."

So the key question is this: Do we really want answers? Or are we more interested in what seems "modern and successful," seeking "good marks and saying the kind of things that win applause?" Do we embody childlike sincerity as we are admonished by Lewis, or do we look more like manipulative teenagers, hungry for popularity? Do we want our arguments to be right and true, or would we rather be politically correct—and "fashionable?"

Do we want our arguments to be right and true, or would we rather be politically correct—and "fashionable?"

Os Guinness, another great apologist of our day, in his book *Time for Truth*, challenges this adolescent tendency to eschew the factual in favor of the faddish: "Truth does not yield to opinion or fashion," he says. "It is simply true and that is the end of it. It is one of the Permanent Things. Truth is true even if nobody believes it, and falsehood is false even if everybody believes it." Thus, both Lewis and Guinness make it clear that confidence in popular thought and accepted trends (i.e., fallacies of *argumentum ad populum*) has very little if anything to do with ideological veracity. Truth is not determined by vim, vigor or a vote.

So if you and I really want answers—if we really want our ideas to be confirmed if they are right and corrected if they are wrong—then perhaps we should humbly set aside our adolescent desire for "good marks" and instead seek what is true (even if it is dreadfully unpopular) and give up what is false (even if it is a dearly loved passion). The integrity of real questions demands nothing less.

> *"Once you were a child. Once you knew what inquiry was for. There was a time when you asked questions because you wanted answers, and were glad when you had found them. Become that child again."*
>
> C.S. LEWIS, *THE GREAT DIVORCE*

Chapter 15

CUTTING THE BABY IN HALF

ONE DAY, AS a king was keeping court, a challenging case was brought before him. There was finger pointing and there were accusations. Anger and confusion prevailed. Tears flowed and emotions were high as two women presented their case before Solomon, the man who was known as the wisest judge on earth.

The dispute was over a child—a young baby boy. Both women claimed to be the mother. Each one expected the judgment to be in her favor. Each one pleaded desperately for the baby to be given to her. Both claimed that the other was lying. Each proclaimed that she alone was telling the truth.

How would Solomon resolve this dispute? How would he administer justice?

The simplicity of his decision was shocking and bold. Solomon in the midst of what seemed to be, at best, 50/50 odds turned to his bodyguard and said: "Take a sword and cut the baby in two. Give one half to each woman."

You know the end of the story. Upon hearing the king's judgment, the real mother cried out, "Please, my lord. Don't kill him! Give him to the other woman." Thus, she proved the obvious: No real mother would let her son be cut in two. For, all that would be left is a dead baby.

There was a time not long ago when an educated person was one who understood the interconnectedness of all aspects of our existence.

As I look at the present state of academia within our contemporary culture, I think of this story. There was a time not long ago when it was assumed that an educated person was one who understood the interconnectedness of all aspects of our existence. One discipline informed the other. Religion and science were interrelated. The humanities were built upon philosophy and vice versa. Economics informed ethics and ethics did likewise for economics. There was harmony between music and math. Faith and learning were intertwined. The university stood for "unity." Professors, preachers, and politicians all knew that a healthy culture was one built upon an integrated body of knowledge—not a segregated collection of disaffected opinions. Truth stood the test of time and withstood the corruption of power. It was self evident that you can't separate faith from facts or belief from behaviors, because both presuppose the other.

Today, however, our post-modern universities seem to be adrift in self-refuting and disconnected claims that fly in the face of the above logic. Tolerance is championed by faculty who won't tolerate those they judge to be intolerant. Diversity is claimed as the highest good by students who openly detest those with whom they disagree. Academic freedom is demanded by the same people who employ "political correctness" to restrict public prayer. The same academician's who railed against government intrusion during the Scopes Monkey Trial, now lobby for a government imposed curriculum that prohibits an open exchange of ideas concerning Intelligent Design—or even Global Warming for that matter. Many scholars now declare that personal life is completely off limits in assessing a man's or woman's fitness for public service. The "content of a man's character" is no longer as important as his political loyalties or professional power.

I wonder, is it possible that in the story of Solomon we find a timely and poignant lesson for today? Here is a question: Are we more like the woman who was willing to let the king cut the baby in half than we are like the one who cried no? As we see postmodern fallacies sawing our culture asunder; separating public policy from personal piety, are we willing to let the king "cut the baby in half" or do we cry, "No"? As we see our schools, our churches, and our campuses constructing false dichotomies that sever our children's personal beliefs from their public behavior, their facts from their faith, and their heads from their hearts, do we tacitly let the king carry out his gruesome work or do we cry, "No—don't cut my child in half"? When we see the consequences of our broken ideas paraded before us on the evening

> *Is it possible that in the story of Solomon we find a timely and poignant lesson for today?*

news in Columbine-like vignettes, do we cry out, "No, I won't let you continue to cut the soul out of my son or my daughter. He needs morality to be a man. She needs piety to have purpose. Please take your sword away. Let my child live."

Solomon knew you couldn't cut a living thing in half and expect it to survive. C.S. Lewis' words of a half century ago call us to heed the same lessons of this wisest man in history. "We have made such a tragic comedy of the situation—we continue to clamor for those very qualities we are rendering impossible... In a sort of ghastly simplicity, we [have removed] the organ [while we continue to] demand the function. We make men without chests and expect of them virtue... We laugh at honor and are shocked to find traitors in our midst. We castrate and bid the geldings to be fruitful."

Scriptures tells us that "Faith without works is dead." Perhaps the lesson of Solomon is that culture emasculated of its character is dead, too.

Chapter 16

TRUTH AND CONFIDENCE: BEING A LIFELONG LEARNER

COLLEGE FOR ME was a starting point—an intellectual and spiritual awakening to a life of asking questions, looking for answers, and seeking direction. It was through the portal of higher education—this "wardrobe" if you will—that I entered a world of adventure, whereby, I began to turn over every stone in the pursuit of something trustworthy and immutable; something true and absolute; something worthy of my commitment and my allegiance. Along the way, I discovered that a classical liberal arts education is one that, in its purest form, pursues all questions with a paradoxical balance of confidence and humility.

Our confidence is in the truth. It is bigger than any one person, one group, or one government. It is an objective and attainable reality. It is permanent and enduring. It is not subject to the ebb and flow of personal opinion or political power.

Truth is the only reliable foundation for liberty, justice, reconciliation, and restoration. Only truth breaks the bonds of oppression. Only truth can bring healing and wholeness to a broken culture and hurting world. Only truth gives us the freedom to bring all ideas to the public square with the confidence that in the end we will keep those ideas that are good and discard those that are bad. History has taught us time and again that without a measuring rod outside of those things being measured we will become subject to the rule of the gang or the tyranny of the individual. Recognizing this, scholars of the ages have confidently given their hearts and minds to the words, "You shall know the truth and the truth shall set you free."

> *Truth is the only reliable foundation for liberty, justice, reconciliation, and restoration.*

Our humility must be in ourselves. We must remember that our Creator "laughs at the wisdom of man," and "our wisdom is no better than His foolishness." Finally, we should not forget that we often tend to think we know all we need to know when, in fact, our humble hearts can help us more than our proud minds.

C.S. Lewis called for intellectual humility as he scolded the self-confident young scholar who was proud of his progressive ideas in *The Great Divorce* by telling him that he was more of a puppet to his own desire for popularity than he was a proponent of independent thinking and superior ideas: "Our opinions were not honestly come by," said Lewis. "We simply found ourselves in contact with a certain current of ideas and plunged into it...You know we just started automatically writing the kind of essays that got good marks and saying the kind of things that won applause." From his own personal experience Lewis knew that the avant-garde intellectual (and don't forget that Lewis knew from whence he spoke) is, more often than not, prone to parrot the party line and, thus, go with the flow, rather than challenge the status quo of what is popular.

But Lewis didn't stop here. He went further to speak of the weakness of misplaced intellectual pride. He challenged the young scholar's tendency to place confidence in the wrong things (in self rather than truth): "[We allowed ourselves] to drift, unresisting, unpraying, accepting every half-conscious solicitation from our desires, we reached a point where we no longer believed." For Lewis the "confidence of unbelief" was not a measure of moral courage or cerebral discipline but rather a sleepy acquiescence to the mesmerizing "solicitations" of what was trendy and in vogue.

All truth is true even if no one believes it, and all falsehood is false even if everyone believes it.

Finally, in transparent self-disclosure, Lewis moves from criticism to solution. He shows the way out. To awaken from the lazy dreams of self-deception, we must return to the honest questions of childhood and humbly look for answers: "Once you were a child. Once you knew what inquiry was for. There was a time when you asked questions because you wanted answers and were glad when you had found them. Become that child again...Thirst was made for water; inquiry for truth." In these words, Lewis echoes the promises of the Sermon of the Mount: "Blessed are those who hunger and thirst for righteousness for they will be filled."

I am a lifelong learner and so are you. My journey and your journey is ultimately one that is guided by the immutable, the permanent and the True, not by the transient constructs of popularity, politics or power. All truth is true even if no one believes it, and all falsehood is false even if everyone believes it. Honesty demands that we boldly pursue ideas that are tested by time, defended by reason, validated by experience and confirmed by revelation. We will only find truth when we place our confidence in it and not in ourselves.

George McDonald tells us in *The Curate's Awakening* that if we want to learn of truth and refute the agnostic within (and isn't there one in each of us?) that we must look to the *Logos*, to Jesus Christ and His way, His truth and His life, and simply do what He tells us to do. Or, in today's vernacular we should simply follow the marketing slogan of Nike™ and "Just do it!" Then, as McDonald says, "In our attempt to obey the words recorded as His, we will see grandeur beyond the realm of any human invention." By humbly becoming a child and yet confidently giving ourselves to the power of Truth we will indeed "see grandeur" and, thereby, move beyond the faddish speculations of man and that much closer to the eternal facts of Eternity.

"We know nothing of speculation. Come and see. I will bring you to the Eternal Fact, the Father of all other facthood."
C.S. LEWIS, *THE GREAT DIVORCE*

Chapter 17

BELIEVE!

This next essay is a commencement address given to Oklahoma Wesleyan University graduates in December of 2008.

I AM PASSIONATE about teaching. I adore learning. I love the Academy and all the ideals that reside within the four walls of the ivory tower.

Let me tell you why…

It's because I am a believer. I believe in education.

I believe that the best education is that which is tested by time, confirmed by experience, validated by reason and, ultimately, grounded in Scripture.

I believe that the Academy is the gate-keeper of our individual virtue and our national conscience. I believe that all intellectual and moral training must be anchored in our Creator who endows us with the rights of life and liberty. And I believe that if we build education on any foundation but Him, we will lose our conscience and shortly thereafter lose our freedom, our joy and our ability to pursue happiness.

I believe that our future lies in the hearts and minds of today's students, and that all cultures are but one generation away from irrelevancy and extinction.

I believe that what is taught today in the classroom will be practiced tomorrow in our churches, our companies, our communities and our country at large.

I believe in absolutes, and I believe that if we don't teach them, learn them and cherish them that we will be cast about by every wave of human desire, political promise, and selfish ambition.

I believe in Oklahoma Wesleyan University because of its mission: A mission set deep in the immutable and unshakable, the permanent and true. Oh, it may not have all the bells and whistles of other schools, but it does have other attributes such as honor, integrity, virtue, temperance or perhaps patience, kindness, goodness, gentleness, faithfulness and self-control.

I believe in OWU because surely there must be more to education than just passing along a few facts and figures and opinions to our young people. Maybe, just maybe, the best education rises above the theories of Dewey and Darwin and Derrida to a way and a truth and a life that is found only in Christ.

I am a believer.

Education has changed my life and it has changed my family. With it God has not only given me a career; but He has opened my mind, changed my behavior, challenged my character, confronted my sin and saved my soul. He has broken the pattern of the generations that preceded me, taken me off of the prodigal path and shown me the joy of choosing the road less traveled. Whether I am poor and unemployed or rich with a predictable paycheck, education is a treasure to me. It has proven to be the gold given by God that serves as His currency for purchasing the incorruptible riches of His Truth.

Today, as you graduate, I leave you with one word: Believe!

Believe in the liberal arts—an education that is driven by the hunger for answers rather than the protection of opinions; an education that is not subject to the ebb and flow of personal agendas or political fads; an education that is not afraid to put all ideas on the table because there is confidence that in the end we will embrace what is true and discard what is false.

Believe in liberty—because the best education is one that indeed liberates. It liberates us from the consequences of those things that are wrong and frees us to live within the beauty of those things that are right.

Believe in integration—and that truth cannot be segregated into false dichotomies, but it is an integrated whole where you cannot and should not separate personal life from private life, the head from the heart, fact from faith or belief from behavior.

Believe in Oklahoma Wesleyan University. Believe in its Mission. Believe in its Message.

Believe in the Primacy of Jesus Christ and that He is the beginning and the end; the way, the truth, and the life; the great I AM; the Word become flesh; Emmanuel—God with us—your Savior and your King, your Lord and your God; the Lion of Judah and the Lamb of God, your Redeemer, your Guide, your peace, your joy, your comfort, your life, your light! Believe that He is risen and incarnate: the Son of God, the Alpha and Omega, the lens of all learning and the Lord of our daily lives.

Believe in the Bible—that it is true, not transient. That it is inspired, not constructed. That it is accurate, not relative. That it is not to be added to nor subtracted from. That it is to be hidden in your heart and proclaimed with your mouth. That it is given by inspiration and breathed by God Himself. That it is the inerrant, infallible, and authoritative written Word of God that guides us in all matters of faith, learning and living.

Believe in Practicing Wisdom—Practice what you preach. Be men and women of integrity. Work out your faith with fear and trembling. Not as though you have already attained all this. If you love Him, you will obey Him. What good is it if you call Him Lord and do not do what He says? Show me your faith without deeds and I will show you mine by what I do. Remember the words of Dietrich Bonheoffer: "Only those who believe obey but only those who obey believe."

Believe in Truth—the Logos—the Tao—the natural law— the revelation of God. Understand that there are self-evident truths that no human being can deny. Believe that such truths are revealed by God not constructed by man, that they are objective and attainable, immutable and constant. Believe that truth gives salvation to the damned and freedom to the slave. Be energized by the unapologetic pursuit of truth. Wherever it leads, be confident in the words, "You shall know the truth and the truth shall set you free." Freedom: the antithesis of slavery. Slavery: the unavoidable outcome of lies—Lies about who we are as people—Lies about what is right and what is wrong—Lies about man and Lies about God.

Today, as you watch the consequences of bad ideas play themselves out on the nightly news, on Pennsylvania Avenue, on Wall Street and on Main Street, be a believer.

Believe in the power of ideas. Recognize the obvious: Good ideas may lead to that which is good, and bad ideas may lead to that which is bad.

Believe in the power of learning and that acquiring the ability to discern between good and bad and right and wrong, actually serves to open the mind rather than to close it.

Believe in the Power of Scripture. Believe in the Pursuit of Truth. Believe in the Practice of Wisdom. Believe on the name of the Lord Jesus Christ and be saved.

Lord we believe—Help our unbelief!

Chapter 18

A ROAD PAVED WITH GOOD INTENTIONS BUT BAD IDEAS

I WAS RECENTLY asked in an e-mail exchange if perhaps I was a bit of an alarmist in my persistent rants about the state of affairs in contemporary academia. (Or perhaps the implication by the writer was that I am just dead wrong?) "After all," said my e-mail pal, "my personal experience with higher education, as well as that of my kids, hasn't been all that negative. Today's colleges and universities aren't as adversarial to intellectual freedom as your writing suggests." Following is a quick response as I offered it to my questioner in case y'all care. (That's Oklahoma slang for: "in case 'any of you' are interested.")

A rule of thumb if I may: When we enter into these kinds of debates, I think we are always wise to start with the bigger ideas. We should go to the top of the funnel, so to speak. This always helps to clarify what is really fueling the argument. It also keeps us focused on the key question, and it helps us avoid distractions as we attempt to distinguish the important from the peripheral, the primary from the secondary, and the false from the facts. In summary, by keeping our eyes on the prize, we avoid rabbit trails in working to separate the wheat from the chaff.

With the target of "bigger ideas" in our sights, I think we first need to vet the ontological and epistemological assumptions of today's academia; for it is, indeed, these assumptions that serve as the guiding paradigms for our institutions of higher learning and these "bigger ideas," I would argue, are much more telling than any of our personal anecdotes. In other words, we need to step beyond our own unique classroom experiences and ask, "What are the school's assumptions about reality (i.e. ontology) and what are the same institution's assumptions about what can be known (epistemology)?"

Nearly all of today's universities fall unabashedly within a post-modern paradigm.

By looking at this bigger picture, we can learn a lot about what is actually guiding a university's mission and message: it's budget priorities, research emphases, publication strategies, and teaching practices.

Research has shown over and over again that nearly all of today's universities fall unabashedly within a post-modern paradigm both ontologically and epistemologically. This is to say that the faculty and administration of most all of our schools of higher learning believe that truth (with a lower case "t") is constructed rather than revealed. They believe that all reality and all corresponding knowledge of what is real are relative and, thus, subject to individual interpretation. They argue that all who trust in the existence of objective Truths (with a capital "T") are either hopelessly ensconced in the fallacious thinking of empiricist modernity or deluded by the black and white buffoonery of the Religious Right. In other words, most of the leaders of today's academic enterprise sincerely believe that the business of the postmodern university is to cultivate a field of opinions and then to assist students in harvesting a crop of malleable social constructs rather than aiding them in pursuing and finding what is objectively true and right and immutable.

For a couple of good sources on this issue of constructivism and its corresponding aversion to a robust, open and "liberal" debate on the nature of truth, knowledge and reality, see Gene Edward Veith's book, *Postmodern Times: A Christian Guide to Contemporary Thought & Culture*, or David Horowitz' *One Party Classroom* and his other, similar work, *Indoctrinate U: The Left's War Against Academic Freedom*. (Note: Before you dismiss Horowitz as some right-wing crank, remember that he was the intellectual engine behind the 1960s radical Left and that he wrote for and supported the likes of the Black Panthers, Tom Hayden and others. Read his autobiography, *Left Illusions,* and you will see that this guy knows from whence he speaks.)

Now if you would like a shorter read, then, at the risk of coming across like a shameless self-promoter, let me refer you to a white paper, *Truth Matters,* published by the Oklahoma Wesleyan University Veritas Worldview Institute and currently available on my website www.EverettPiper.com. This is a summary of the prodigal path of today's academia, and in it you will see several real-world examples that corroborate my claims of a post-modern moral malaise on today's campuses.

Finally, after reading the above and the sources I cite and thinking through the corresponding anecdotes of your own educational experience, I encourage you to go to David French's book, *A Season for Justice*, and perhaps then to Jim Nelson Black's white paper titled, *I Will Not Be Silent*, or to Black's corresponding book, *The Freefall of the American University*. And if you still need more convincing that something is terribly amiss in academia, and that we, as learners, have essentially become a bunch of feckless frogs in Kohlberg's kettle of moral meandering (Forgive me for that one but I just couldn't resist), you could go to the *University of Michigan 2002 Course Catalogue*, which openly states in its description for a course titled "Ethics of Corporate Management" that it "is not concerned with the personal moral issues of honesty and truthfulness" because it is assumed that all students attending the U of M have already "formed their own standards on these issues." Here you see the poster child of my point. With post-modern confidence (a contradiction in terms?), one of the premier academic institutions in our land proudly teaches that "honesty and truthfulness" are relative constructs subject to the whim of the individual. Then, the leaders of this university, along with all the rest of us, wonder with righteous indignation (or is it relative indignation?) why their alumni with prestigious diplomas hanging on their office walls at Enron, Fannie Mae, Freddy Mac and AIG are liars, cheats and crooks? Go figure...

By keeping our eyes on the prize, we avoid rabbit trails in working to separate the wheat from the chaff.

So, back to the question: Yes, I am claiming that today's universities are hopelessly muddled in a swamp of opinions where the guy with the loudest voice or the most obnoxious attitude or the most prestigious diploma wins the day and controls the debate regardless of the veracity of his claims. Indeed, there are many faculty members who are polite and, in spite of their affection for post-modernity, do allow students to express their views freely. But for every one of these kinder and gentler post-mods, there are literally hundreds of elitists who sincerely believe that they are justified in not tolerating those they deem to be intolerant. They seem proudly to say that they "hate those hateful people" and that they are "sure that nothing is sure" and that they "know that nothing can be known." Do you feel like you are watching a dog named "Self-Refuting" chase his tail a bit here?

All ideas have consequences.

I know, I know...all of us have some positive stories to tell about our trek down the *"via del la alma mater,"* but shouldn't we challenge ourselves to look beyond the wandering road of our subjective existentialism and critically evaluate the intellectual paradigms that serve as the map for today's educational journey? All ideas have consequences. All ideas lead somewhere; and, frankly, road signs are all around us that warn of the negative fruit of post-modernity. Like Digory in Lewis' *The Magician's Nephew,* we see the witch standing before us with the red juice of an intoxicating fruit dripping from her lips, and we hear her triumphantly declare, "Do you know what this fruit is? I tell you it is the apple of [subjectivity], the apple of [power], I know for I have tasted it...You and I will both live forever and be queen and king of this whole world..."

Digory instinctively knew that he should ignore the witch's temptations because she spoke of her rules and not Aslan's. Likewise, we must know that when we begin to define our own standards and laws, when we become the authors of what is honest and what is trustworthy, when the truth becomes a construct of man rather than a revelation of God, it is then that we become "as God" and, thereby, travel the road of original sin over and again as did our ancestors before us. These ancestors likely now know the final destination of all roads paved with good intentions and bad ideas.

Chapter 19

NARCISSUS AND ECHO

YOU ALL KNOW the story. Narcissus was the son of the river god Cephisus. He ran in the foothills and forests of Greece. He joined with the fawns and dryads in the woodland sports as they ran the streams and climbed the mountains. He was incredibly handsome, so handsome indeed that the beautiful nymph Echo followed his every step, pursuing his love.

One day after an exceptionally good hunt, Narcissus was running through the woods and came upon a calm, clear pool carved out in the bend of a river. Exhausted and fatigued, he stooped down to take a drink and saw his own image in the water. Struck by the beauty of the reflection, Narcissus stood by the fountain's edge gazing with admiration at his own beautiful form. He said to himself "Ah—neither Bacchus nor Apollo themselves surpassed such allure as mine."

With infatuation, Narcissus reached out to embrace his own reflection. He could not tear himself away. He lost all thought of food or rest. He just stayed by the river's edge, day after day, hovering over the pool, gazing at his own image.

As time went by, the fire he cherished consumed him more and more. He lost his color, he lost his vigor, he lost his strength; until one day in one final attempt to embrace his own fading beauty, Narcissus leaned over the edge of the pool, fell in, and drowned.

In love with himself, Narcissus died, leaving nothing but the faint hint of Echo's voice in a distant valley as she mourns the loss of such wasted beauty.

This story came to mind recently when I was confronted by a fellow political junkie who disagreed with what he defined as my conservative worldview. His comment went something like this: "The problem with you conservatives is that you are arrogant. You think you have all the answers. You think you are always right."

It isn't the degree of confidence that distinguishes one "believer" from another, but rather it is the source of confidence.

Now I have a point of clarification and then a question.

First, clarification: The difference between conservatives and progressives is not that conservatives think they are right and others don't. To the contrary, any healthy debate presupposes that one person believes his or her ideas are right while contending that another person's ideas are wrong. By definition a disagreement assumes mutual dissent. Common sense (as well as Webster) tells us that a dispute involves arguing one thesis against another. Both parties think they have the correct answer. Both are confident in the accuracy of their position. Both believe the other person's ideas are mistaken. Wouldn't it be a silly waste of breath to disagree if we had no confidence in the "rightness" of our own position and the consequent "wrongness" of opposing views?

Surely we can agree that liberals, progressives and conservatives are equally confident in thinking they have the better ideas. It seems obvious that my friend who claimed to be "right in criticizing those who claim to be right" needs to remember that one accusing finger pointed at others is often outnumbered by several fingers pointed back at oneself.

So, it isn't the degree of confidence that distinguishes one "believer" from another, but rather it is the source of confidence. One person will claim there is no final answer. All truths are merely the consequence of social constructs and human preference. People are the source of their own truth. Another person disagrees and says that truth is bigger than this. It is an objective absolute beyond our ability to create. It is out there. It is real. It is given from above and revealed on the heart. Thus, the real difference is that one man claims to be the source of truth while the other claims to be its recipient.

It isn't arrogant, after all, to fall in love with something bigger than oneself.

Now, my question: Why is it arrogant for one person to say, "I don't have all the answers but I believe there is one;" and yet humble for another to proclaim with narcissistic confidence that "There is no final answer. Truth is what I decide it is. I am the final judge. I am the final arbiter of what is right or wrong, true or false, beautiful or ugly"?

Perhaps we should remember the story of Narcissus. As we try to make sense out of the clamor of competing ideas and political agendas, do we find ourselves satisfied with the sound of our own "beautiful" voice or do we hear a faint echo mourning the loss of things that we know to be pure and true, honest and good? As we stand at the edge of the pool of competing worldviews, do we find ourselves staring lovingly at our own image, our own opinions, tastes, preferences and desires, or do we look deeper, beyond our image, as if "seeing in a glass darkly" seeking to someday "know even as we are known"?

Maybe it would serve us all well to take a humble look in the mirror as a reminder that it isn't arrogant, after all, to fall in love with something bigger than oneself.

Chapter 20

A TRAIN TO SOMEWHERE

LAST CHRISTMAS I was watching the movie *The Polar Express* with my sons, Seth and Cobi. As you likely know, this film is a digitally animated, 3D production that stars Tom Hanks as the conductor of a train (the Polar Express) that takes its passengers on a magical Christmas Eve trip to the North Pole. All along the way, the children on the journey must decide if they "believe" in Christmas. One boy, in particular, has his doubts. The train ride represents his struggle: Is Christmas real or is it just make-believe?

At the end of the movie, the little boy is trying desperately to determine what to think of his adventure. What should he believe? What is true and what is false? The conductor, Tom Hanks, then turns to the boy and says, "The one thing about trains: It doesn't matter where you're going. What matters is deciding to get on."

As I watched this movie, I thought of today's academia. More specifically, I thought of the paradigm called "postmodern constructivism" that prevails on most of today's campuses. This model asserts that reality is simply "made up" (constructed) by individuals in conversation with one another. There is no Truth with a capital "T" but only personal "truths" that are uniquely created by each individual as the culminating synthesis of tolerance and dialogue. It is the journey that matters, not the destination. The constructivist's goal is to build a personal belief system, not to seek and discover immutable facts. There is no such thing as a final answer. It really doesn't matter what worldview you choose as long as you choose one. To travel is better than to arrive. Just "get on" a train—any train.

> *A truly liberal education is one that indeed liberates.*

Historically, there has been a better way. Yes, education does involve dialogue and a discussion; and, of course, we do build knowledge on the foundation of experiences. However, a classical liberal arts education (one that is validated by nearly 1,500 years of tradition) is more than just the process of choosing from a smorgasbord of personal values and various worldviews.

> *Education, at its best, serves as a light to those who are in the dark.*

A truly liberal education is one that indeed liberates. It liberates mankind from the consequences of those things that are wrong and frees us to live within the beauty of those things that are right. Education that is grounded in the pursuit of Truth, as opposed to the constructions of man, will ultimately free you and me from the oppression of lies. Education, at its best, serves as a light to those who are in the dark. It is a map to those who are lost. It is a law to those who want order. When we are driven by the hunger for answers rather than the protection of opinions, we are not afraid to put all ideas on the table because we have confidence that in the end we can embrace what is true and right and discard what is false and wrong. Confident in the existence of Truth, we recognize that we should find the right "train" that is going in the "right" direction.

In the 1990s there was another movie, a historical drama that also featured a train ride. This train, however, was not leading to the magical, snow-filled skies of the North Pole but instead, to the mysterious and ash-laden winter of places such as Auschwitz and Dachau. The movie was Stephen Spielberg's *Schindler's List,* and in this film we see it does, indeed, matter which train one chooses to get on. The obvious fallacy of post-modern constructivism comes alive before our eyes. Who can watch fellow human beings herded as cattle into boxcars bound for the furnaces of the Nazi prison camps and argue that it doesn't matter where the train is going? Who would dare tell the Jews that the joy is in the journey and that the destination is of little consequence? It is apparent that some "trains" lead to good places and some "trains" lead to places that are evil. It is painfully obvious that we all want to avoid getting on the wrong train. Hopefully, our hearts cry out with Oscar Schindler's as he weeps for those who have been forced to get on the wrong train—headed to the wrong place.

> *Education represents the path we have chosen for eternity.*

As an educator, I am passionate about learning and I am passionate about ideas. Ideas have tremendous potential and power. Ideas are always directional: They have consequences. Education, thus, is not stagnant, and it definitely does represent a journey that will take us somewhere. With our ideas, we are going in one of two directions: either toward the forgiveness and freedom that only God's revelation can offer or toward the bondage that always and inevitably results from man's "constructions." In this context, education represents the path we have chosen for eternity.

Perhaps the Psalmist says it best: "Teach me your ways O Lord and I will learn...to walk in your Truth." Our ways always result in slavery, treachery, and oppression. God's ways always lead to liberation and freedom: "You shall know the truth and the truth shall set you free." Ideas matter. When we get on the right train and go in the right direction, we can celebrate and sing, "Free at last. Free at last. Thank God Almighty, I am free at last!"

Chapter 21

A DEGREE IN OPINIONS

SOMETIMES ABSURDITY IS the best teacher. Like a firm slap, it can shock the senses. Like the alarm on your nightstand, it can break the power of nightmares, awaken us from illusion, arouse us from dreams, and call us back to reality. The ridiculous juxtaposed with the rational can indeed be a most effective tool in showing the clear difference between the two.

Let me illustrate.

I want you to suppose that you are a brand new college student. You have just enrolled in your first semester at Oklahoma Wesleyan University (or OU, OSU or TU—for that matter). You have selected an academic major. You are excited about your classes. You have met all your professors, purchased all your textbooks, reviewed all your syllabi, and taken note of all your assignments. Your goal of getting a university degree is now at hand. You are finally a college freshman and you are ready to learn!

Now walk with me down this path a bit further. It is four years later. You have made it. You have read countless assignments. You have written innumerable five-page papers. You have taken all your tests, passed all your quizzes, and delivered several impromptu speeches. You have just completed your last finals week and the day has come. You are enjoying commencement ceremonies. You have done it. You are about to graduate!

You can't pretend to be educated if all you have is an opinion. There are objective facts. There are indisputable truths that serve as the foundation for any meaningful educational experience.

As president of the university, I finish my commencement address—something you will never remember because it was too long and I should have known better. The time you have been waiting for has come. All the graduates stand and approach the platform as they are called by their academic divisions: first arts and sciences, then philosophy and religion, then business, then humanities, etc.

Now it is your turn. Your name is called. The academic dean gives you your honors cord. Your family is in the audience cheering. You walk toward me: you wearing your academic regalia and mortar board and I am wearing mine. We join in a vigorous handshake as I give you your long-awaited diploma and say, "Congratulations! You now have a degree in opinions."

After four long years of study, after eight semesters of classes, after so many assignments, so many late nights, so many tests, so many debates and after so much work directed toward mastering a body of information relevant to your major and minor; after sitting through countless lectures on such diverse topics as the classical truths of literature, the ethics of leadership, the rules of accounting, the laws of physics, the *summum bonum* of philosophy, and the unalienable rights cited in the Declaration of Independence and guaranteed by the Constitution; I have the audacity to hand you a diploma and say, "It really doesn't matter what you believe as long as it works for you. Here is your degree in opinions!"

This is truly ridiculous. The absurdity is obvious. For we all know that you didn't go to college to major in "whatever" or to get a degree in "opinions." To the contrary, you went to college to gain knowledge and to acquire at least some level of mastery of the truths relevant to your major and minor as well as the broader disciplines implicit in the liberal arts curriculum.

You went to college to learn something, and your diploma represents the acquisition of such knowledge. When it comes down to it on commencement day—your opinion really doesn't matter, nor does mine. What matters is quite simple: Did you learn the facts and figures, the theories and the truths that were required of you? Do you now know more about geological science than you did when you started? Have you learned the difference between credits and debits and can you balance a ledger? Do you understand the ethical assumptions implicit in the march for civil rights?

Opinions can be dangerous, self-centered and cruel.

Can you pass the MCAT because of your knowledge of human biology? I am being blatantly rhetorical here for obvious reasons. You can't pretend to be educated if all you have is an opinion. There are objective facts. There are indisputable truths that serve as the foundation for any meaningful educational experience. Getting a degree requires learning such truths, not simply holding to your opinions. To claim otherwise is silly. It is—well—absurd.

I was recently reading the works of contemporary scholars such as Michel Foucault, Richard Rorty, and Jacques Derrida who argue that there is no such thing as objective truth and that all knowledge, all values, all morality, and all ideas of right and wrong, good or bad, are merely the products of an ongoing "community narrative" or social dialogue within a "global village." They say that truth is a construct not a precept. It is a conversation not a conclusion. Truth is really not true, you know. It's all relative. It's all a matter of opinion.

We need to ask ourselves: Do we really believe this, and are we willing to live with the consequences of such ideas?

"A just law squares with the moral law or the law of God."

Martin Luther King, Jr., was once asked why he believed it was right to break the law of the land in his effort to promote civil rights and social justice. How could he justify breaking some laws and yet advocate obeying others? In his famous "Letter from a Birmingham Jail," he answered his critics: The answer lies in the fact that there are two kinds of laws. There are just laws and unjust laws. One has not only a legal but a moral responsibility to obey just laws. Conversely, one has a moral responsibility to disobey unjust laws. And what is a just law? King responded: "A just law squares with the moral law or the law of God."

King understood something that perhaps we would all do well to remember. Opinions can be dangerous, self-centered and cruel. They indeed are used to justify all kinds of unjust things. Only that which rises above the selfish constructs of the human mind can set the stage for freedom and dignity, liberty and justice. King knew that there was a revelatory truth, a natural law, which served as the only solid foundation for human value, civil rights, justice, freedom, and racial liberation. He also understood very well that man's opinion is inevitably clouded by selfishness and deception, and, thus, sets the stage for the powerful to construct systems of oppression over the powerless.

Maybe what is right and wrong, good and bad, pure and profane is ultimately measured by degrees of truth rather than degrees of opinion after all.

Chapter 22

THE PRODIGAL PATH OF ACADEMIA

HERE IS A STORY we all know. It is about a young man who left home and spent his days traveling to the places of his wildest dreams. He spent his nights pursuing his own way and doing what he wanted. But in the end, he spent countless private moments wishing he could just go home. Reflect with me as I recount this young man's tale.

Once there was a prominent rancher who had a son. Even though this son was very well-cared for and had everything he needed, he approached his father one day and said: "Father, I don't want to wait for my inheritance. Frankly, I am suffocating living at home under your rules and your expectations. I want my freedom. I want my money. It is time for me to move out of the house, get my own place, and live as I want."

Well, the father was broken hearted, but he relented. He gave his son the freedom he demanded. He let his son decide how to use (or abuse) his own inheritance and go his own way.

So the son packed his bags and left. He moved to the city and got his own apartment. There, undisciplined and dissipated, the son squandered everything he had. He had his freedom. He had his money. And, he wasted it all by living his own way.

About the time the son was spending the last few dollars of his inheritance, the economy really went south and a severe recession occurred. The son was hurting. Having nothing left, this young man began living on the streets and scavenging in back alley dumpsters. He was so hungry he was now eating garbage in an effort to survive.

Well, this finally brought him to his senses, and one day he said, "All the ranch hands back home working for my father are much better off than me. They at least sit down to three meals a day, and here I am starving to death. I am going back home."

This story of the prodigal son causes me to reflect on today's colleges and universities.

I think of higher education's "birthright and inheritance" as seen in the original mission statements of many of our nation's seminal institutions: Of Harvard's *Christo et Ecclesia*, "For Christ and the Church;" of Princeton's *Vitam Mortuis Reddo*, "I restore life to the dead;" of Yale's expressed goal for its students "to know God in Jesus Christ and…to lead a godly, sober life."

I consider academia's prodigal path where public and private colleges and universities across our land, contrary to their founding creeds very similar to those cited above, have recently implemented administrative sanctions and even outright bans on certain student religious groups. Such action, thereby, has effectively excluded traditional and historical orthodoxy from being openly discussed and freely debated on their respective campuses.

I look upon faculty members who have been denied tenure because they dared to assume they could engage in an open and "liberal" exchange of ideas on matters such as intelligent design, climate change, and sexual politics.

I grieve at the consequences of a many young adults "living their own way," of eating from "back alley dumpsters," of the routine reports of drug addiction, binge drinking, date rape, sexual abuse, escalating suicide rates, and the pandemic nature of STDs on today's campuses.

I, also, think of our Father, His provisions and His teachings, of Veritas, of "Truth," of Harvard's early affirmation on its school shield: "If you hold to my teachings...you shall know the truth and the truth shall set you free."

Has "having our own way" resulted in what we expected when we told our Father we wanted to move out of His house?

Finally, I think of "home" and its safety, security, and the true freedom we have under our Father's roof as opposed to the subjugation we experience in the house constructed of our own delinquency and rebellion.

In the original story of the prodigal son we are told, "That not long after squandering his birthright, there was a bad famine in the land and the son began to hurt. Having nothing left but his "own way," this young man began working in the fields to slop pigs just to survive. He was so hungry he was now eating the corn-cobs in the pig slop.

I don't know about you, but as an educator who has degrees from three different universities similar to those cited above, I look at the academic world in which I now live, and I have to ask myself a few questions. Has "having our own way"

Is it possible Dad was smarter than we thought He was all along?

resulted in what we expected when we told our Father we wanted to move out of His house? Did we get what we wanted when we spent our inheritance? Is our chosen path as much fun to traverse as we hoped? Have "our wildest dreams" led us to where we expected or have we stumbled into a nightmare, wading in fields of pig slop and eating the "corncobs" of abuse, dysfunction, selfishness, and addiction? Did we get the freedom we hoped for when we left home, or have we actually become slaves to the consequences of frivolous spending and childish irresponsibility?

One last question: Is it possible that Dad was smarter than we thought He was all along?

Perhaps it is time for us to leave the corncobs behind and go home.

Chapter 23

TWO ROADS

Two roads diverged in the yellow wood,
And sorry I could not travel both
And be one traveler, long I stood
And looked down one as far as I could
To where it bent in the undergrowth...

I shall be telling this with a sigh
Somewhere ages and ages hence:
Two roads diverged in a wood, and I –
I took the one less traveled by,
And that has made all the difference.

ROBERT FROST, "THE ROAD NOT TAKEN"

WHILE REFLECTING ON this classic poem by Robert Frost, I can't help remembering a recent conversation I had with a good friend and fellow Michigan State University Spartan. It was one of those fun times where the hours flew by like minutes, where disagreement was serious and sincere, yet cordial and honest—where confidence was tempered with compassion and both parties likely shared the proverbial hope that "as iron sharpens iron, one man sharpens another." The bottom line was this: We each held views—strong views—that were essentially opposite. I believed and expressed one idea with great conviction. He did likewise, but to the converse effect. He advocated one ideological course. I espoused yet another. We disagreed. This is the kind of wrestling that good education is made of.

Is the truth of God real and, if so, how can we know it?

In our debate both my friend and I moved from one idea to another, sparring and jockeying for position. But, in the end, all of our arguments basically came down to one key question. Is the truth of God real and, if so, how can we know it?

After way too much time elapsed, both of us realized that we had to move on to other things. My friend, thereby, concluded by calling for a truce. He said, "I think there are many paths up the mountain, but the beauty is that they all lead to the summit. Perhaps we shouldn't argue so much about which road we choose and agree that it isn't the specific path that's important, but rather the journey."

As iron sharpens iron, one man sharpens another.

Now, on the surface, this argument seems quite attractive. Surely the path isn't nearly as important as the destination, is it? If we go to the left or to the right, we all will end up in the same place won't we? Clearly, the winding road is just as good as the straight one; the broad gate just as worthy as that which is narrow. And doesn't respect for tolerance and diversity require us to embrace all ideas, all values, all lifestyles, all worldviews, and all paths, as essentially equal?

These same questions were addressed recently in a Q and A session of the Veritas Forum at Harvard University by the Indian-born philosopher, Ravi Zacharias. After his presentation (whereby he argued for the knowable, absolute and exclusive nature of God's truth), Dr. Zacharias was confronted by a student who contended that all religions are the same. All lead to the same place. All have equal theological, ontological and epistemological veracity. There are many paths up the mountain.

There are many paths up the mountain, but only One Person made a path down the mountain to love us and show us the way.

Zacharias' response was pointed as he paraphrased the poet Stephen Turner: "[Indeed] all religions are the same except for their understanding about the character of God, of the cosmology and meaning of the universe, of human nature, of human value, of the nature of reality, of ethics, the good life, charity and kindness, sexuality, suffering, joy, hope, salvation, and our eternal destination of either heaven or hell."

Yes, indeed, all worldviews are the same, except in matters critical to life and death, social and physical health, temporal and eternal existence, etc. Hmm—I guess if you set these minor issues aside then all roads do lead to the same place.

In her book, *Finding God Beyond Harvard,* Kelly Monroe Kullberg builds upon the truth implied in the sarcasm of

Zacharias and Turner. She says, "[Yes] there are many paths up the mountain as the saying goes. But we find that only one person made a path down the mountain from the top, to love us [and show us the way]."

Do we really believe that all paths lead to the same destination or does common sense tell us that if you want to get from point A to point B, it is wise to get a map and follow a guide? Maybe choosing to follow the One who shows the way, who knows the right path, and who exemplifies the right ideas will help us avoid getting lost.

As we begin each new day with all its hope and promise, perhaps we would all do well to reflect on the words of Robert Frost, and remember that as we approach the diverging cultural roads before us, choosing the one less traveled does make all the difference.

Chapter 24

SEGREGATION VERSUS INTEGRATION

"What you have just seen is the difference between those who voted on the basis of religion versus those who voted on the basis of science."

RON REAGAN, 2004

THIS QUOTE COMES from the son of former president Ronald Reagan. It was on the night of the 2004 presidential election, and Ron Reagan was serving as a political commentator for CNN. As the polling booths closed and the nation's votes were being counted, a major newsflash was developing. It was the story of the "values voters"—the millions of people who said in the exit polls that morality, social standards, and, yes, even religion had been a determining factor in their respective votes. It was a story about "red states" vs. "blue states." In Ron Reagan's opinion, it was a story about science vs. religion.

I am using this quote of Ron Reagan's to go in a direction that is perhaps unexpected. I don't want to talk about politics. Instead, I want to talk about education.

Stay with me for a minute while I explain.

When Ron Reagan looked in the camera on that November night in 2004, he was visibly discouraged. He was honestly chagrined that so many people would permit their personal values and/or their respective religion to actually influence their political opinions and consequent vote. Ron Reagan in fact was disgusted. That night, as I sat in my living room watching his commentary, it was apparent that he simply couldn't believe that in the modern era, an election could be swayed by a bunch of uneducated, red-state buffoons who actually think religion has a place in the public square.

Ron Reagan's key premise was this: Religion is a private matter. Believe what you want but don't confuse your personal faith with scientific facts. The head and the heart must be kept in separate spheres, segregated if you will, so that we never use religion to inform our science or science to inform our religion. Do your church thing on Sunday but don't bring it to work on Monday, and by all means, don't ever let your faith and any corresponding personal values influence anything you do in the voting booth, in the workplace or in the classroom.

Education that separates facts from faith, head from heart, and science from religion ultimately falls short.

Now let me ask a couple of questions as I try to bring us back to the issue of education.

Do you believe this model of separating the head from the heart, fact from faith, science from religion is the best route to becoming a truly educated person? Or does your instinct tell you that we somehow lose the benefits of synergy and the magic of unity when we protect one set of ideas from another and, thereby, contrive the conversation to fit our own preconceived notions of what is right or wrong, true or false? Do you believe that we are standing alone as islands unto ourselves, or does your personal experience tell you something different: That nature, humanity, society, culture, and the world-at-large are somehow tied together by a common thread of certain inalienable rights and God-given responsibilities and endowments—what C.S. Lewis called the Tao? Do you believe in the segregation or integration of ideas?

I thought of these questions and the corresponding story of Ron Reagan recently when a friend asked me to explain why I am so passionate about Oklahoma Wesleyan University (OWU) vs. Michigan State University (MSU), one of my alma maters. My response was something like this:

"I believe you can get a good education at Michigan State (I know— I am a Spartan). But the real difference between OWU and MSU is that we at OWU seek to teach our students to think about biology, psychology, math, and business from the context of a comprehensive and unified 'Truth.' Education is never complete if it ignores the verity that all truth is an integrated whole. Education that separates facts from faith, head from heart, and

The best education teaches us to confront the false dichotomies of our day.

science from religion ultimately falls short. The best education teaches us to confront the false dichotomies of our day. Good education becomes great when it emboldens us as a community of learners to demand that our faith informs our facts and our facts inform our faith."

So, I have to admit, yes, I am one of those red-state folks who believes that my religion should influence my daily reality and that my faith should permeate and guide everything I think, say and do.

Yes, I am ignorant enough to believe that science and religion both lead to the same end.

And finally, yes indeed, I am one of those uneducated buffoons who believe that the best education is one that instinctively eschews segregation of all kinds and, conversely, embraces the integration of all ideas as nothing about which to be discouraged or angry.

Chapter 25

IDEAS HAVE CONSEQUENCES

AT A TEXAS ACADEMY of Science Annual Meeting, the keynote speaker for the event was the 2006 Distinguished Texas Scientist, Dr. Eric Pianka, who currently serves as the Cooley Centennial Professor of Zoology for the University of Texas. Professor Pianka holds a B.A. from Carleton College, a Ph.D. from the University of Washington, and another doctorate from the University of Western Australia. His responsibilities include teaching undergraduate courses in biology and ecology. Dr. Pianka has received the Teaching Excellence Award for his work in the classroom. He is a well-known author, environmentalist, and conservationist.

Someone with such impeccable credentials is exactly the kind of teacher you would want for your 18-year-old son or daughter as he or she heads off to college—right?

Before you answer this question too quickly you might, first, be interested in hearing a bit more about Dr. Pianka's acceptance speech.

To set the stage, let's go back to the Texas Academy of Science's annual event. After arranging for the videographer to turn off his camera, the professor stepped to the podium and began his remarks by castigating anthropocentrism (the idea that human beings hold a privileged position within the universe). He proceeded to say that people are no better than bacteria and that mankind holds no superior status among the biological byproducts of evolution. Finally, he claimed that by virtue of our overpopulation we are guilty of destroying the planet. Dr. Pianka declared to his audience that the earth will likely not survive unless drastic measures are taken to correct this problem. If the earth is to endure, he says, the present human population must be reduced by as much as 90%.

Yes, you read correctly. This scholar, this professor from one of our nation's largest and most respected universities, believes that in order to save the planet—to conserve the earth and its environment—it would be a good thing to get rid of nine out of every ten people. (By the way, the means for accomplishing this depopulation cannot be natural death or birth control. This would take too long. Pianka's solution is disease: Specifically the spread of the airborne Ebola virus. I'm not kidding. He really suggested this.)

What we believe always guides what we do.

Now the story of Professor Pianka may seem extreme, perhaps even absurd. But please don't get distracted by this absurdity. Don't go down the rabbit trail of what might be a natural aversion to the messenger, and, thus, risk missing the real point to this story. Instead, I encourage you to focus on the message and ask a few basic questions.

Specifically, ask yourself questions about the likely consequences of Pianka's ideas. For example:

1. What are the consequences of ideas that declare human beings to be mere biological products of a primordial soup—organic material essentially without moral value?

2. What are the consequences of ideas that subjugate human life to the greater good of planetary maintenance?

3. What are the consequences of ideas that deconstruct self-evident truths that have served since the dawn of time as the foundation for human dignity, the sanctity of life, and the basis for inalienable human rights?

4. What are the likely consequences of ideas that postulate truth to be the mere product of dialogue and a cultural construction—a political consensus?

5. And finally, what are the consequences of ideas that declare people to be "no better than bacteria" with the obvious conclusion that a virus should be allowed to thrive just as much, if not more so, than human beings?

During my 27 years of serving as a leader of multiple academic institutions, I have argued repeatedly that ideas have consequences. I have suggested over and over again that what we believe always guides what we do. I have attempted to demonstrate that you can't separate the head from the heart, fact from faith, attitudes from actions, virtue from values.

You can't separate the head from the heart, fact from faith, attitudes from actions, virtue from values.

Ideas matter. Companies, churches, families, and neighborhoods—people in general—are unavoidably blessed or cursed by their guiding principles—by the import of their ideas. In many ways, we inevitably do practice what we preach.

In his classic work, *Ideas Have Consequences,* Richard Weaver contends that the cure for the ills of any given culture lies closely at hand in the "renewed acceptance of an absolute reality and in the recognition that ideas [result in consequent behaviors]." In making his point, Weaver goes further and quotes Carlyle: "But the thing a man does practically believe...the thing a man does practically lay to heart, and know for certain...is in all cases the primary thing for him, and creatively determines all the rest."

Ideas serve as the impetus for all human action.

Yes, that "thing" that ultimately "determines all the rest" is the power of ideas. Ideas serve as the impetus for all human action. Ideas lead the way to good and evil, love and hatred, beauty and destruction. Ideas fueled the fire of the Renaissance and ultimately stemmed the tide of the Bolshevik Revolution. Ideas have opened Hell's doors whereby we have seen slavery, prejudice, Auschwitz, and the Killing Fields. Ideas have likewise led us through the grand gate of emancipation, brotherhood, sacrifice, and love. Ideas are never neutral. They always lead somewhere. They always have consequences.

So, as your son or daughter prepares for college, ask yourself a couple of questions: What dreams do you have for them and the generations to come? What ideas do you hope will govern their lives, their families, and their culture? Finally, ask yourself this: Would you trust your 18-year-old at the knee of Dr. Pianka?

Chapter 26

VALUES, VIRTUES AND VACUUMS

ONE THING I LEARNED early in my career is the principle of the vacuum. As it is in physics, so it is with human nature. Nothing will always be filled with something. Just like a vortex in the Pacific, a black hole in the cosmos, or the Hoover in your living room, so it is in the boardroom, the public square or the church foyer. A vacuum simply can't be resisted. Nothingness cannot sustain itself. Rest assured a void will be filled. In the absence of goodness, cruelty thrives. Where there is no love, hatred prevails. Those without humility are inevitably arrogant. Take away integrity and gossip runs rampant. Without vision the people perish, and on and on it goes.

This principle came to mind recently as I was reading an editorial in *The Philadelphia Inquirer* written by Dinesh D'Souza, the Rishwain Research Scholar at the Hoover Institute at Stanford University. D'Souza contends that the best explanation for the present world crisis of Muslim rage directed toward the West is not the commonly accepted argument of clashing religions, i.e., of Islam vs. Christianity. To the contrary, he believes that Islam's rage is not directed toward true Christianity but instead toward radical secularism and the moral vacuity that faithful Muslims see therein.

Here is a bit of D'Souza's argument:

Nothing will always be filled with something.

"It is time to revisit some common assumptions. Many Americans consider Islamic fundamentalists and Christians as essentially equivalent, 'kindred spirits' in the words of the late novelist William Styron. Al Gore finds in President Bush 'the American version of the same fundamentalist impulse that we see in Saudi Arabia.' In her book *The Mighty and the Almighty*, Madeleine Albright frets that 'hard-liners can find in the Koran and the Bible justifications for endless conflict.' ...As Jim Wallis says in his book *God and Politics*, there is a close parallel between Islam's holy war against the West and George Bush's holy war against Islamic terrorism. From this perspective, the best solution is for America to stand up for the principles of secularism and oppose both Muslim and Christian fundamentalism."

D'Souza continues: "...not only is this diagnosis of the problem wrong, but the solutions proposed are actually fueling Muslim rage and making future terrorist attacks against us more likely. The reason is that, from the point of view of Islamic radicals, America is not hated because it is Christian. Rather, America is hated because it is secular, what Osama bin Laden has called 'the leading power of the unbelievers.' So, by promoting [radical] secularism, we are corroborating the charge of radical Muslims that we are the enemies of their religion, and this also alienates traditional Muslims and pushes them into the radical camp."

Dr. D'Souza goes further and emphasizes, "Islamic radicals...make their case against America and the West not on the grounds that [our] cultures are Christian, but on the grounds that [we] have abandoned Christianity. In his May 2006 letter to President Bush, Iranian President Mahmoud Ahmadinejad faulted America not for being Christian, but for not being Christian enough. Many years earlier, the radical theoretician Sayyid Qutb made the same point [criticizing that] in the modern era, 'religious convictions are no more than a matter of antiquarian interest.' Other Muslim radicals today echo these arguments. The influential Pakistani scholar, Khurshid Ahmad, leader of the Islamic Assembly of Students argues: 'Had Western culture been based on Christianity, on morality, on faith, the language and modus operandi of the contact and conflict would have been different. But that is not the case. The choice is between the divine principle and the secular materialistic culture.'"

*History has shown time and again that
the absence of good always leads
to the manifestation of evil.*

And so on and so forth. D'Souza argues, as he concludes: "Thus the popular notion that the war against terrorism is a battle of two opposed forms of religious fundamentalism is false. This is not why the Islamic radicals are fighting against America. From the perspective of bin Laden and his allies, the war is between the Muslim-led forces of monotheism and morality vs. the American-led forces of atheism and immorality.

Secularism, not Christianity is responsible for producing a blowback of Muslim rage."

Now you may disagree with some of the assumptions implicit in D'Souza's argument of Koranical tolerance (For example he seems to sidestep the Muslim hermeneutic of the doctrine of abrogation and doctrine of deception). But don't get distracted by this and miss the forest for the trees.

Instead, think for a moment of the principle of the vacuum—that unavoidable law that you know and experience on a day by day basis—the rule of replacement that says nothingness always draws something into its void. Consider how history has shown time and again that the absence of good always leads to the manifestation of evil. Think about D'Souza's basic premise that Muslim malevolent ill will and Islamic hatred is being drawn irresistibly into your own backyard by a vacuum—a vacuum of values, a vacuum of virtue. Then ask yourself this question: Does the emptiness of secularism give you more comfort than the fullness of timeless truths and objective revelation?

Chapter 27

THE CONSEQUENCE OF A GOOD IDEA

Written February 23, 2007 in honor of the 200th anniversary of William Wilberforce's successful efforts to bring an end to the slave trade in all of the British Empire.

OVER THE PAST couple of years as I have been writing for Crosswalk.com, *BreakPoint Worldview magazine,* Bullypulpit.com, The Oklahoma Council for Public Affairs and Politicalmavens.com, I have argued repeatedly that ideas have consequences. I have stated over and over again that what we believe always guides what we do, that you can't separate the head from the heart, fact from faith, attitudes from actions or virtue from values. For good or for ill, ideas matter. People are unavoidably blessed or cursed by their guiding principles—by the import of their ideas. In many ways we inevitably do practice what we preach.

"[That] thing a man does practically believe...the thing a man does practically lay to heart, and know for certain...is in all cases the primary thing for him, and creatively determines all the rest" (Carlyle).

People are unavoidably blessed or cursed by their guiding principles—by the import of their ideas.

In my columns I often tend to lean toward waving a flag of danger and, thus, warning of the bad ideas and the bondage and the dysfunction they bring. I have warned of the dehumanizing effects of radical Darwinism, and I have bemoaned the selfishness of post-modern amorality. I have challenged that we should beware of the constructed "choices" of man and be very leery of hedonism's uncanny gift of deception. Week after week, I have attempted to craft a story that at least hints a bit at the destructive consequences of what M. Scott Peck calls "the diabolical human mind" and of history's tendency toward insanity and seduction.

But today I would like to focus on the power of a good idea, one that bore its fruit on the streets of London some two hundred years ago on February 23, 1807. The idea was simple, timeless and profound. Its promoter was a young British Parliamentarian named William Wilberforce. And here was his idea: God is God and we are not.

Wilberforce believed that all men and women are created equal. He argued that regardless of age, race, size, shape, intelligence or mental acumen we all have unalienable rights granted by our Creator; that we all are made in the image of the invisible God; that slavery, which was the backbone of the

British economy at the time, is the desecration of such an image, and that by enslaving one man under another, the owner is claiming to be God. Wilberforce's idea was this: No one has the right to define what is human and what is not. This is God's alone to judge.

For two decades, Wilberforce fought tirelessly in the British Parliament for his idea. He was beaten back time and again. He was ridiculed. He was accused of economic treason. He was insulted. He was ostracized. His political career suffered and was all but lost. His influence waned and his voice was muffled. But he held fast to his idea. He relentlessly pursued it, defended it and promoted it. He believed in its power. He boldly declared that he would not be silenced. He confronted the "corruption...of human nature" and called "vice and wickedness" by their true names. He refused to accept the politically correct definitions of sin and contrasted the self-justifying talk of "frailty and infirmity, occasional failings and accidental incidents" with what he called the "humiliating language of true Christianity"—the call for personal repentance, spiritual regeneration and moral responsibility.

Wilberforce believed passionately in a biblical worldview. He was confident in it as the only solution to the corruption of politics and the evils of oppression. He, however, did not advocate imposing his views with force. To the contrary, he believed in the power of persuasion and the example of personal integrity. He wrote that Christians should "boldly assert the cause of Christ in an age when so many who bear the name of Christian are ashamed of Him. Let them be active, useful, and generous toward others. Let them show moderation and self-denial themselves." Thus, he made it clear that his ideas would only prevail if they were grounded in and proven by the lives of those who espoused them.

The power of an idea lived out in humility, balanced with integrity and measured with grace can indeed change the world.

Wilberforce concluded (knowing that he could commend belief but not command it) by saying, "The national difficulties we face result from the decline of religion and morality among us. I must confess equally boldly that my own solid hopes for the well-being of my country depend, not so much on her navies and armies...as on the persuasion that she still contains many who love and obey the Gospel of Christ. I believe that their prayers may yet prevail."

After arguing for over 20 years on the floor of the British Parliament, William Wilberforce celebrated victory on February 23, 1807. It was the victory of an idea, not one of political or military conquest but that of a good idea over a bad one.

It was a victory of truth over lies, of freedom over slavery, of sanctification over sin.

Ideas do indeed matter and in this case we see that the power of an idea lived out in humility, balanced with integrity and measured with grace can indeed change the world. In his example, Wilberforce leaves us with this hope: The "prayers of many who love and obey the Gospel of Christ...may yet prevail."

Chapter 28

THANKSGIVING AND PRAISE

A Thanksgiving Day message written in November 2007.

AS A CONSERVATIVE, I believe there are certain truths that should be left untouched. Like a good wine, some ideas simply get better with age. They have stood the test of time and have been defended by the measure of reason. They have been confirmed by revelation and validated by experience. Yes, indeed, some ideas have been so rigorously vetted and are so well stated that they should simply be honored, left unedited, and approached with humility, in the present age as they were in the past.

Like a good wine, some ideas simply get better with age.

Today, please indulge me as I suggest that we have one of those ideas before us. As we celebrate this holiday weekend, I think we are all well served to return with a somber spirit to the original words that led to the last Thursday in November being recognized as a national day of "Thanksgiving and Praise."

Here are those words:

"The year that is drawing towards its close, has been filled with the blessings of fruitful fields and healthful skies. To these bounties, which are so constantly enjoyed that we are prone to forget the source from which they come, others have been added, which are of so extraordinary a nature, that they cannot fail to penetrate and soften even the heart which is habitually insensible to the ever watchful providence of Almighty God.

"In the midst of a civil war...which has sometimes seemed to foreign States to invite and to provoke their aggressions, peace has been preserved with all nations, order has been maintained, the laws have been respected and obeyed, and harmony has prevailed everywhere except in the theatre of military conflict...

"Needful diversions of wealth and of strength from the fields of peaceful industry to the national defenses, have not arrested the plough, the shuttle, or the ship; the axe has enlarged the borders of our settlements, and the mines, as well of iron and coal as of the precious metals, have yielded even more abundantly than heretofore. Population has steadily increased, notwithstanding the waste that has been made in the camp, the siege and the battlefield; and the country, rejoicing in the consciousness of augmented strength and vigor, is permitted to expect continuance of years, with large increase of freedom.

"No human counsel hath devised nor hath any mortal hand worked out these great things. They are the gracious gifts of the Most High God, who, while dealing with us in anger for our sins, hath nevertheless remembered mercy.

"It has seemed to me fit and proper that they should be solemnly, reverently and gratefully acknowledged as with one heart and voice by the whole American people. I do therefore invite my fellow citizens in every part of the United States, and also those who are at sea and those who are sojourning in foreign lands, to set apart and observe the last Thursday of November next, as a day of Thanksgiving and Praise to our beneficent Father who dwelleth in the Heavens. And I recommend to them that while offering up the ascriptions justly due to Him for such singular deliverances and blessings, they do also, with humble penitence for our national perverseness and disobedience, commend to his tender care all those who have become widows, orphans, mourners or sufferers in the lamentable civil strife in which we are unavoidably engaged, and fervently implore the interposition of the Almighty Hand to heal the wounds of the nation and to restore it as soon as may be consistent with the Divine purposes to the full enjoyment of peace, harmony, tranquility and union."

ABRAHAM LINCOLN, OCTOBER 3, 1863

Yes—some ideas simply stand alone; strong, secure and enduring: "Thanksgiving and Praise to our beneficent Father...offering up the ascriptions justly due to Him for such singular deliverances and blessings...humble penitence for our disobedience, and fervently imploring...the Almighty Hand to heal the wounds of the nation."

Some ideas simply stand alone; strong, secure and enduring.

Some ideas need no rebuttal. No debate is appropriate. No response seems right other than one coming from a humble and contrite heart full of "Thanksgiving and Praise."

Chapter 29

DO YOU BELIEVE IN EVIL?

Written following the horrific shootings at Virginia Tech. April, 2007.

I WANT TO ask you a question. Do you believe evil exists?

These past few days, while watching the endless reporting on CNN, MSNBC, and FOX News about the rampage of Cho Seung Hui at Virginia Tech, did you feel as if you were a spectator to something gone terribly wrong? As you read the countless news articles about this week's massacre, did you conclude that you were witnessing something blatantly and unequivocally immoral? Did you know in your heart that you were watching and reading about something explicitly and absolutely beyond the pale, something that was utterly bad, something that was categorically evil?

Let me dig a bit deeper.

When you looked into the eyes of Cho as he leveled his 9 millimeter Glock point blank in your direction (thus, giving you the exact view of the last thing 32 of his victims likely saw as they faced their own death) did you see anything objectively bad? When you listened to this young man's rant as he read his disjointed and venomous last words and testament, what did you think? When he exonerated himself of any responsibility and, thus, blamed those whom he was about to kill by saying, "The decision was yours. Now you have blood on your hands that will never wash off," what did your conscience tell you?

Did you find your own blood running cold and were you nearly speechless—as was one Virginia Tech junior who, after viewing Cho's video, said "I saw his picture on TV and when I did I just got chills...There are really no words"?

Did something well up inside you and did that "still small voice within" join in the chorus of our culture and scream, "What is wrong with us? What is this world coming to? Somebody do something! After Columbine, after Paducah, after Nickel Mines, after Oklahoma City, after 9/11, after endless terrorist bombings and Islamic celebratory beheadings, please do something! Moral neutrality be damned. This just has to stop!"

After this week's news, do you really believe that there is no such thing as right or wrong, good or bad? Do you really buy the claim that it doesn't matter what you believe—as long as it works for you? Do you seriously accept the academic arguments of our day that pedantically preach that objective truths actually don't exist and any position on values, virtues, morality, good and evil, is, after all, simply a personal construct relative to the individual or to the culture which claims it?

The most empirically proven fact in history is the very existence of sin.

Do you believe this stuff or do you see in the face of Cho the consequences of post-modernity's love affair with self and our resulting infatuation with making the rules up as we go, with constructing truths rather than obeying them, with killing the prospect of God rather than honoring His hope and precepts?

After this week, what do you think? As you look deep into the eyes of Cho, what does your heart tell you? Do we have it right? Can man achieve utopia on his own? Do we have the goodness within ourselves to develop our own systems of morality without the boundaries or restrictions of any absolute standards? Do we have real liberty without the limits of law and can that license be granted without the selflessness of servitude?

Do you believe all is well in the world and the progress of humankind is marching boldly in a positive direction? Or, in the shadow of April 16, do you see something that your instincts have told you was there all along? Is the difference between good and bad real? Do right and wrong exist? Do justice and injustice, life and death, morality and immorality, vice and virtue have objective definitions beyond matters of personal opinion? Does the human heart have the propensity to choose poorly and to do despicable things, because the most empirically proven fact in history is the very existence of sin?

Do you believe in evil?

Now, ironically, I think that if your answer is yes, you actually have more hope than those who say no. If you admit that an absolute wrong is in fact real, don't you have to agree that there must be an absolute right? If objective badness exists, doesn't there also have to be objective goodness? Isn't the only measuring

The image of Lady Justice tells us that judgment must presuppose objectivity.

rod of evil, the reality of an unchanging and immutable standard of good? Without a *Logos,* a Tao, a Word and a Way beyond you and me, how would we know or recognize those things we call wrong, unfair, bad, or evil? Wouldn't the very discussion be meaningless?

The image of Lady Justice tells us that judgment must presuppose objectivity. The scale must be something beyond that which is being weighed.

Take courage and confidence in the absolute
GOOD...It is only in this goodness that
we find any objective basis for civilization,
for sanity and for our salvation.

Consider this: If you and I are the final measure of our own morality then when it all comes down to it, we cannot evaluate the moral rightness of any action at any time for any reason. The logical end of such narcissism has to be a futile nihilism that looks back into the eyes of Cho Seung Hui and says, "Who am I to judge?"

Do you believe in Evil? Have you been watching absolute EVIL raise its ugly head in unrestrained celebration in recent days, and have you said to yourself, "Shooting kids in schools is wrong; flying planes into buildings is appalling; bombing open air markets is unjustified; and celebrating the beheading of your adversaries is not a personal moral construct. These are atrocities and they have to stop!"

If this is your heart's cry, then take courage and confidence in the absolute GOOD that you have just implicitly embraced. Surely it is only in this *goodness* that we find any objective basis for civilization, for sanity and for our salvation.

Chapter 30

JOSEPH KONY'S "INVISIBLE CHILDREN"

DO YOU KNOW who Joseph Kony is? If you don't, let me give you a brief résumé.

Address: Northern Uganda

Education: Primary school dropout

Marital Status: Polygamous, with 27 wives (at last count)

Children: 42 (that are reported)

Occupation: Self-styled mystic prophet who believes he is a spirit medium, hearing and channeling the voices of dead Chinese generals and many others who tell him to rape, pillage, plunder, and abduct his own people for the sake of a revolution that stands for "righteousness and justice."

Accomplishments: He has successfully established a guerilla movement that has avoided detection, prosecution or defeat for the past 20 years. Over this timeframe, he has utilized multiple strategies to abduct and enslave over 20,000 children to serve in his "Lord's Resistance Army." These "soldiers" at 10-to-12 years of age will, upon command, carry out grizzly acts of butchery, murder, gang rape and other unspeakable atrocities.

Kony has employed witchcraft rituals to brainwash thousands of these innocent young kids to believe such absurdities as any bullet fired at them in the field of battle will turn to water. He has beaten his wives for not having his bath water ready and ordered the mutilation and murder of his spouses' families. He has plundered and attacked hundreds of villages, destroyed thousands of crops and left field upon field fallow and barren. His regime has been responsible for bringing the entire northern regions of his country to a virtual standstill as families cower in fear and thousands of orphans migrate covertly on a daily basis, trying to avoid becoming the next front line of "soldiers" in his locust-like "army of god."

The mantra of our day: "It doesn't matter what you believe as long as it works for you," just doesn't work.

Honors and Citations: He has attained the noteworthy accomplishment of being indicted by the International Criminal Court (ICC) for crimes against humanity, which specifically include murder, enslavement, sexual enslavement, rape, cruel treatment of civilians, pillaging, inducing rape, forced enlistment of children into rebel ranks, and abducting girls to offer them as rewards to commanders.

References (maybe not positive, but they are references): Tens of thousands of Ugandan youth now officially known as the "invisible children" are hiding in their country's wilderness and back alleys in an attempt to avoid Kony's forced conscription. These elementary school-age kids literally sleep in trees at night to avoid being attacked and eaten by hyenas and other wild animals. During the day, they turn the tables and try to follow feral dogs so that they can steal their prey in order to have something to eat. These innocent-faced, beautiful, young children are constantly moving from one shadow to another in their attempts to stay alive within some measure of freedom and sanity.

Worldview: In the fashion of quintessential, post-modern constructivism, Kony responds to the International Criminal Court saying, "I have done nothing wrong." He practices a syncretistic, Druze-like religion, where he melds together the theology of his liking and, thus, serves his megalomania and moral relativism by reciting the Rosary on Sunday, praying the Al-Jummah prayer on Friday, using witchcraft Monday through Thursday and spending the 30 days of Ramadan fasting.

Non-judgmental tolerance is a ruse.

Okay, I have said it before, and I will now say it again: Ideas matter. Ideas have consequences. The mantra of our day that proudly declares, "It doesn't matter what you believe as long as it works for you," just doesn't work. When you juxtapose our contemporary cultures' infatuation with cross-cultural "tolerance" against the predictable outcomes of such maniacal evil as that of Joseph Kony, you quickly cringe at the unavoidable conclusion: Non-judgmental tolerance is a ruse. Worldviews are indeed not morally equal. They can't be. Otherwise, we are logically forced to admit that the raping and brainwashing of 10-year-olds is indeed fine "as long as it works for you." If all values are personal; if all virtues are nothing but social constructs; if all morality is the result of an ongoing conversation; if everything we hold to be right and all that we believe to be wrong is nothing more than the result of political power plays and popular vote; then all you or I can do in response to the cries of the "invisible children" is shrug our shoulders and say, "Who am I to judge?"

Tolerance actually has some limits after all and those limits are found at the boundaries of Truth.

So, if you believe in justice; if you want mercy for yourself and seek to be an instrument of it in service to others; if you listen to stories such as that of Joseph Kony and you have any sense of indignation and feel that perhaps you have just looked into the very eyes of evil; then ask yourself this question: Why? What is "in you" that causes such a reaction? What measure and rule seems to rise up from within and say, "No! This is wrong?" Is it simply "what works for you" or is it something a bit stronger and more permanent, something more enduring, immutable and real? Is it possible that what works for Joseph Kony is indeed irrefutably and absolutely wrong because it violates that very thing in your heart that you know to be beyond your opinion or mine or his? Is it possible that tolerance actually has some limits after all and those limits are found at the boundaries of Truth?

Chapter 31

PLAYING GAMES

IN THE 1940s, Richard Weaver wrote a book called *Ideas Have Consequences*. Over the course of subsequent decades, many scholars have come to agree with Weaver's seminal premise: Ideologies, values, beliefs and propositions do indeed influence community health, interpersonal vitality, and human behavior. To try to separate public life from private life, beliefs from behaviors, head from heart, fact from faith, or attitudes from actions is somewhat akin to a farmer talking about a harvest while ignoring the obvious importance of seeds. Ideas germinate and grow and bear predictable fruit. As a kernel of wheat has the potential to produce amber waves of grain, so will ideas inevitably bear the good fruit of love, joy and peace or the bad crop of hate, revenge and war. All human action, for good or for ill, starts with the power of the smallest seed—the seed of an idea.

A recent trip to the mall caused me to think about the fruit inevitably born of ideological seeds. As I walked past a bookstore replete with magazines promoting gossip and slander, I couldn't help wondering about the consequences of these ideas.

As I hurried past a clothier selling teenage sex more so than shirts, shoes, and jeans, I had to ask myself the question: What are the consequences? As I sauntered up to a video game store and looked in the window at the numerous games featuring overt violence, implicit rape, anarchy and mayhem, I had little choice but to worry about the consequences of such images. Do any of us really believe that a diet of poison will somehow produce a healthy body? Do we honestly think that vice has lost its power over the human heart? Have we somehow concluded that the billions of dollars spent on marketing have no bearing whatsoever on our propensity to buy the product being sold?

> *Ideas germinate and grow and bear predictable fruit.*

Over the past couple of years, all of us have watched the evening news and have been appalled by story after story of school violence across the land. Duane Morrison took six girls hostage at Platte Canyon High School in Bailey, Colorado. He held them captive for hours, molesting them and fatally shooting one of the girls before turning the gun on himself. Two days later, Eric Hainstock took two guns into his school in Cazenovia, Wisconsin, and exacted revenge on his principal. He shot him several times. The principal died en route to the hospital. Charles Carl Roberts took 10 girls hostage in an Amish school in Nickel Mines, Pennsylvania. When the police interrupted his plans to sexually molest the girls, he killed five of them execution style and then shot himself in the head and died. And who can forget the shootings at Columbine, Paducah, and Virginia Tech?

Recently, Rodney Walker, spokesman for Rockstar Games, makers of Grand Theft Auto—a video game known for giving its young players the "thrill" of shooting pedestrians and police officers alike while also rewarding any astute young hacker with a sexually explicit scene hidden within the program—defended his company by saying, "Some people like our games and some don't. We can't try to beat these arguments...we have to let the game speak for itself. We just want [you] to know this is just entertainment."

Just entertainment?

Is it just entertainment for a teenager to lock himself away with his PlayStation and feed on a constant diet of murder, theft, and voyeurism? Is it just entertainment for that young man to enjoy vicarious violence and valueless sex more than a good book or a healthy relationship? Is it just entertainment for any of us to prefer the debased rather than the divine? When we chose to put images in our minds and ideas in our hearts that swirl and churn into an insatiable appetite for more violence, more gossip, more hatred, and more debauchery, is it just entertainment? Were these things just entertainment for Morrison, Hainstock, and Roberts, or did the ideas they indulged in so voraciously bear predictable and inevitable consequences? Did their beliefs prompt their behaviors? Did their attitudes betray their actions? Was their private life an indicator of things to come as they acted out in public?

The ideas and images that we "entertain" do indeed have consequences.

Nearly 2,000 years ago it was said that a "good man brings good things out of the good stored up in him, and the evil man brings evil things out of the evil stored up in him. For out of the overflow of the heart the mouth speaks" (Matthew 12:34-35). Many of us know another version of this timeless axiom. We learned it at our grandmother's knee: "Garbage in–Garbage out."

The ideas and images that we "entertain" do indeed have consequences. Perhaps we should follow the advice of Mr. Walker from Rockstar Video and "let the games speak for themselves."

Chapter 32

THANK YOU, DAN BROWN

WITH OVER 43 MILLION people having read Dan Brown's *The Da Vinci Code,* many are asking questions. Who is Jesus? Was he simply a political zealot who was executed by the Romans? Was he the husband of Mary Magdalene and the father of the royal bloodline of France? Did Jesus claim he was divine or did the church fabricate this story simply to protect its political power? What does history truly tell us about Jesus?

Because so much of western civilization has turned on the axis of Christianity, the import of this question seems obvious. The phenomenal numbers associated with *The Da Vinci Code* certainly imply that people do indeed want to know: Who was this man? What should we believe?

If truth exists, we shouldn't be afraid of pursuing it.

Frankly, Dan Brown is right to prompt these questions. None of us should blindly accept what we are told without being willing to weigh the evidence. Our goal should be to find the facts, not protect our opinions. If truth exists, we shouldn't be afraid of pursuing it. As I have said before, the best education is one that puts all ideas on the table with the confidence that, in the end, truth will win as we embrace what is right and discard what is wrong.

Good history is grounded in facts and bad history is built on fabrications.

With this said, I think we should thank Dan Brown.

We should thank him for reminding us that good history is grounded in facts and bad history is built on fabrications. Any honest student knows that the quality of one's research is only as good as the data one collects. So, thank you, Dan Brown, for showing us that eyewitnesses are more trustworthy than those removed from the story by 2000 years and that Hollywood is likely more interested in faddish agendas than factual presentations.

We should thank Dan Brown for pushing us to investigate our past. If we do as Brown suggests and return to the original Christians, we are led to a place unexpected by *The Da Vinci Code's* own premise. In the first century Church, we meet men and women seeking to find the truth—not hide it. We see people uninterested in political power, personal gain and physical comforts. We are led to the door of those who believed in and gave their lives for an idea: an idea of peace and restoration, an idea of goodwill and redemption, an idea of grace and forgiveness. We find people who believed in an objective standard because they knew it protected mankind from the evils of self-deception and the horrors of self-destruction. Thank you, Dan Brown, for reminding us that there were thousands who believed Christ was exactly who He claimed to be and gave their lives as proof of their belief.

We should also thank Dan Brown for shining a light on the dark corners of certain worldviews and, thus, showing us that all philosophies do not lead to the same end. Some worldviews lead to love and others lead to hate. Some clearly lead to dialogue and others are deaf to argument and persuasion. Some promote peace in the face of disagreement, and others wish to harm those with whom they disagree. Thank you, Dan Brown, for giving the body of Christ an opportunity to show that it doesn't riot in the streets, burn embassies or issue death warrants when offended by the way its leader is depicted in a book, a movie, or a cartoon.

So, in my opinion, we owe Dan Brown a note of thanks. He has done us a huge favor by focusing our attention exactly where it should be—on one of the most important questions of all time.

Thank Dan Brown for pushing us to investigate our past.

History, as well as the nightly news, reminds us that from the coliseums of Rome, to the streets of Riyadh, to the boulevards of Richmond, Jesus is much more than a good teacher, wise sage or religious prophet. Believers through the ages have found the proof of Christ's claims in the changed lives of people who follow Him. George MacDonald says it best: "In our attempt to obey the words recorded as His, we see grandeur beyond the realm of any human invention." As we see our own lives being restored and redeemed, we have all the evidence we need to declare along with MacDonald that "we cast our lot with those of the Crucified."

Ideas matter. *The Da Vinci Code* rightly invites us to consider a very important idea and one with wide-ranging consequences. I am thankful for anyone, Dan Brown included, who encourages us to discuss what history and human experience truly tell us about the idea of Jesus.

Chapter 33

DEFENDING PULLMAN? LET THE MAN SPEAK FOR HIMSELF

I WAS INVOLVED in an email exchange regarding the 2007 movie *The Golden Compass* whereby one of Phillip Pullman's defenders (a person who claims to have read all three books of the trilogy, *His Dark Materials*) said the following: "Pullman is anti-organized religion, but I do not see him as anti-God or anti-Christian, and his comments seem to have no agenda...I really liked the books...I never read them as being anything more than a 'quest.'"

Well, rather than challenging this with my own words let me cite a better source: Pullman himself.

Here is Pullman's direct quote from a recent interview:

"Underlying the trilogy there is a myth of creation and rebellion... [This myth] depicts a struggle: the old forces of control and ritual and authority, the forces which have been

*embodied throughout human history in such phenomena as
the Inquisition, the witch-trials, the burning of heretics, and
which are still strong today in the regions of the world where
religious zealots of any faith have power, are on one side; and
the forces that fight against them [are on the other]...So, for
instance, the book depicts the Temptation and Fall not as the
source of all woe and misery, as in traditional Christian
teaching, but as the beginning of true human freedom—
something to be celebrated, not lamented. And the Tempter
is not an evil being like Satan, prompted by malice and envy,
but a figure who might stand for Wisdom."*

Not anti-church, anti-God, and anti-Christian? No agenda?
In one succinct paragraph Pullman manages to do the following:

1. He disparages all of faith and blatantly exaggerates
   negative stereotypes of the Church to make it emblem-
   atic of all that is wrong and evil.

2. He uses thin and juvenile arguments against the Church
   by fallaciously aligning all the mistakes of Christians,
   i.e., witch burnings, inquisition, etc., with the sum total
   of Christianity. (This is akin to saying that because I
   have met some bigots in the South that all southerners
   are bigots.)

3. He admits that he intentionally reverses good and
   evil/God and Satan and makes "the Tempter" the
   personification of freedom and joy and "God" the
   purveyor of gloom and oppression.

4. He even is so bold as to say that the temptation that led
   to the fall is not the cause of all that is bad, but is
   instead the beginning of all that is to be celebrated!!!

So I say again—let Pullman speak for himself. *The Golden Compass* and the two books that follow it are explicitly anti-God, anti-religious and anti-Christian written by an author who enjoys the Orwellian gymnastics of reversing traditional definitions and putting mankind in the position of God and God in the position of a killjoy (that ultimately needs to be killed!!!). Kind of sounds like the original sin doesn't it?

No agenda? I don't know about you, but Pullman sure seems to think there's one.

Chapter 34

BRASS OR CLAY: EXTREME MAKEOVER PART 1

These next two chapters were written in 2006 while partici-pating with helping an area family selected by ABC Television's *Extreme Makeover Home Edition* program.

ABOUT A YEAR AGO, a Baptist pastor from Dewey, Oklahoma, died at 48 years of age. A heart attack took his life, leaving his wife and ten children (five still at home) with very little. No house. No retirement. No college fund. Some would say John White died and left his family with nothing.

Don't believe this for a minute; it just isn't true. To the contrary, John White left his family and friends something of incredible value: He left them his character, his faith and his integrity.

It was exciting when ABC's *Extreme Makeover Home Edition* selected the White family to be the subject of an upcoming episode. Over the course of five days, while the Whites were on vacation in the Florida Keys (courtesy of ABC), hundreds of volunteers went to work building a 5,000 square-foot house, a new barn, and a guest cottage. College scholarships were given. Furniture was donated, as well as landscaping, artwork, and interior design. All of this was the talk of the town.

> *"Brass is more easily mistaken for gold than is clay."*

In watching all the excitement, I thought often of C.S. Lewis' statement: "Brass is more easily mistaken for gold than is clay." You see, Lewis recognized the human tendency to be attracted to shiny and beautiful things. Given a choice, people obviously want wealth rather than poverty, health rather than illness, and pleasure rather than pain. We all prefer the comfort, stability, and strength of brass rather than the grit and fragility of clay. And to be quite frank, brass is pretty while clay is ugly. Things such as houses, scholarships, vacations, and the glitter of recognition and self-importance are so attractive. Compared to all this, who among us sees much joy in the dirt of life; the ordinary and routine? We all want a good life, a better life.

Now don't misunderstand me. I am not suggesting that these desires are necessarily wrong, nor is Lewis. In fact, in *The Weight of Glory,* Lewis challenges us by suggesting that we wish for too little not too much:

> *"If there lurks in the most modern minds the notion that to desire our own good and earnestly to hope for the enjoyment of it is a bad thing, I submit that this notion has crept in from Kant and the Stoics and is no part of the Christian faith. Indeed if we consider the unblushing promises of reward and*

the staggering nature of the rewards promised in the Gospels, it would seem that our Lord finds our desires not too strong, but too weak. We are half-hearted creatures, fooling about with [temporal things] when infinite joy is offered us, like an ignorant child who wants to go on making mud pies in the slum because he cannot imagine what is meant by the offer of a holiday at the sea. We are far too easily pleased."

It isn't our desire that is misplaced. It is our satisfaction. We are far too easily pleased with temporal things and, in our contentment, we fail to aspire to what is eternal. We are satisfied with the brass of life and we fail to remember the repeated lessons of childhood. Presents are forgotten quickly. Brass tarnishes. Its beauty fades. It isn't gold.

It isn't our desire that is misplaced. It is our satisfaction. We are far too easily pleased with temporal things and, in our contentment; we fail to aspire to what is eternal.

The real story of the White family is a story about character not a cottage, it is about faith not funds, and it is about giving not getting. The gold in this story is John White's integrity. When we looked around and saw all the "good works" being done, we saw the fruit of a man's character not only providing for the needs of his family but blooming into a wonderful harvest as hundreds experience the blessing of putting themselves last so that someone else could be first.

So, don't believe for a second the report of John White leaving his family with nothing. This couldn't be farther from the truth. John left his family with everything. And in doing so he taught us all a lesson. We should never be too easily satisfied with the brass of life, but we must only be content in possessing the gold. Brass is temporal. Gold is eternal. Material comforts last for but a season; but faith, hope and love last forever. This is a truth that John now enjoys in its fullness.

Material comforts last for but a season; but faith, hope and love last forever.

Permit me to take a bit of liberty with another C.S. Lewis quote:

"John White's earthly life was only like the drawing, like the penciled lines on flat paper. It vanished in the risen life only as pencil lines vanish from the real landscape, not as a candle flame that is put out but as a flame which becomes invisible because someone has pulled up the blind, thrown open the shutters, and let in the blaze of gold; the golden sun."

Chapter 35

THE ISLAND OF DUFFLEPUDS: EXTREME MAKEOVER PART 2

"For what stood in the doorway was Aslan himself, the Lion, the highest of all High Kings. And he was solid and real and warm and he let her kiss him and bury herself in his shining mane. And from the low, earthquake-like sound that came from inside him, Lucy even dared to think he was purring."

C.S. LEWIS, *THE VOYAGE OF THE DAWN TREADER*

IN THE *CHRONICLES of Narnia*, C.S. Lewis tells some wonderful stories that are rich with spiritual allegory. *The Lion, the Witch and Wardrobe* is a powerful tale of the ultimate sacrifice. *The Last Battle* brings us face to face with Sovereignty and Providence. And *The Magician's Nephew* draws us into the musical harmony of creation. I have come to love these books as I read them time and again to my two boys over the years.

Recently, one story in particular has caught my attention. It is *The Voyage of the Dawn Treader*. In this book we join Edmund, Lucy, Eustace and Prince Caspian as they set sail across the Great Easter Ocean in a ship called the Dawn Treader. On their journey they visit several islands, one of which is inhabited by invisible creatures called Dufflepuds. These imperceptible troublemakers threaten to go to war with Caspian unless the prince and his crew agree to help lift the magic spell that has made these phantoms invisible. They claim that the only way to reverse this spell is for Lucy to enter the magician's house, scale the stairs that lead to the second floor, find the Book of Incantations and read the "spell to make hidden things visible." The Dufflepuds demand that Lucy do this, and she, in fear and trepidation, complies.

Well, as Lucy reads the spell from the magician's book, the Dufflepuds become visible, and she discovers that this unseen menace is really nothing more than a group of harmless and amusing dwarfs—not at all the threat they were assumed to be.

Our perceptions and our fears do not have any bearing whatsoever on God's constant presence.

But there is more. As Lucy turns to leave the magician's room, she sees something standing in the doorway before her. It is Aslan—the Lion—the highest of all High Kings, the son of the Emperor from across the Great Sea. Lucy cries with delight and runs forward saying, "Oh Aslan, it is kind of you to come."

"I have been here all the time," says Aslan. "You have just made me visible."

As I read this story, I am reminded of a timeless truth: Our perceptions and our fears do not have any bearing whatsoever on God's constant presence. When we fear the unknown, He is here. When the unseen challenges of life press in upon us, He is here. When the demands of others seem threatening and unfair, God is here. When things seem frightening and beyond our control, when the "Dufflepuds" rant and intimidate and when we are forced to scale stairways that are dark and shadowy, God is not some distant power that visits only upon occasion. "Aslan" has been and is "here all the time."

In March of 2006, I and several of the Oklahoma Wesleyan University students, faculty and staff had the privilege of being involved in the television program *Extreme Makeover, Home Edition*. Here is a story from "backstage," if you will.

In the final hours of our endeavor to construct a 5,000 square foot house in less than seven days, the contractor who was associated with the *Extreme Makeover* story came to me sheepishly and asked a question. It went something like this: "Dr. Piper, did you happen to see the big backhoe that we brought in for the demolition work?" When I said no and looked perplexed he asked more pointedly: "Did you see the shovel on the front of the backhoe?" My confusion forced him to go further and explain. He said, "Well, when we brought in the backhoe, it had dirt on it from the previous project because we hadn't washed it off." He then looked at me with tearful emotion and said, "I can't explain it, but the dirt on the shovel of the backhoe had an image on it. It was clearly the shape of the face of Jesus."

God is never far away from us.

By reading the "Book of Incantations" and doing what it said,

Lucy found that Aslan had been with her all the time. Likewise, my new *Extreme Makeover* friend found that by obeying the biblical admonition to give selflessly, the body of Christ came alive before his very eyes and he began to see Jesus—even in the dirt on a shovel.

God is never far away from us. We just need to "make him visible" through our prayers, through our faith and by our obedience to His way, His truth, and His life.

> *"The angels keep their ancient places,*
> *Turn but a stone and start a wing.*
> *'Tis ye, 'tis your estranged faces,*
> *That miss the many-splendored thing."*
>
> FRANCIS THOMPSON, *IN NO STRANGE LAND*

Chapter 36

THE LESSON OF BLUE

"Me and you and dog named Boo
Travelin' and a livin' off the land.
Me and you and a dog named Boo
How I love being a free man."

LOBO, 1971

DO YOU REMEMBER this 1970s ballad?

I think of it often as I watch my boys play with their black Labrador retriever named Blue (We goofed—We mistook Lobo's pronunciation of his wandering partner's name).

It reminds me of simpler times—of AM/FM radios—of summer camp—of teenage friends—of a dog's loyalty—of "me and you and a dog named Blue."

I also think of higher ideals—of the joy that comes from adventure—of the majesty of creation—of life and liberty—of "travelin' and livin'off the land."

But most of all, as I hum this tune in the back of my mind, as I watch my sons tussle with and play fetch with their dog, "Blue," I think of freedom—the internal compass and natural hunger that all of us share—the longing to be "a free man."

Freedom is not free. It always comes with a cost.

You see, Blue has taught me something very interesting about freedom. Freedom is not free. It always comes with a cost.

Permit me to illustrate.

If you have ever owned dogs, you know of their natural love for the outdoors, for hunting, for retrieving, for a good run. You can almost see the laugh in a Labrador's eyes when she sees you are about to let her off her leash—when she knows she is about to romp in the fields or swim in a lake, or roam in a local woods until exhausted. She absolutely loves freedom.

But you also know something else about dogs. They can never be let loose of the restrictions of a chain, the confines of a kennel or the boundaries of a back yard until they have first acquired discipline.

A dog can never enjoy "freedom" until she learns to obey. Oh, your dog may be "free" to ignore you and your commands. She may be "free" to walk away rather than sit, stay, heel, or come. She may be "free" to defy any rules or restrictions you try to impose on her. She may be "free" to think she is the master and you're not. But this is really a story of sadness not of joy because you know that in her ignorant and stubborn way of living your dog is not experiencing a fraction of the freedom that could be hers. You know that if she would just listen, simply accept some boundaries, and just obey your commands, you could and would let her go. She wouldn't even need a fence or a tether anymore if you could trust her to stay out of the road and away from traffic. She could have total freedom and the run of the property if she would obey some basic rules established for her own good and stay away from things that you know could kill her.

The payment for liberty is always found in the currency of submission.

The simplicity of a dog's life—the lesson of Blue—has shown me over and over again that the benefits of freedom cannot be enjoyed without first paying the price of obedience. No *one* or no *thing* experiences the "gain" of emancipation without first submitting to the "pain" of correction. Good things always cost something. We must remember that the payment for liberty is always found in the currency of submission.

Recently, Dr. Russ Hittinger of the University of Tulsa, in commenting on the paradox of Natural Law and human freedom, said something like this: Freedom is a direct consequence of Natural Law. Our understanding of Law and our compliance therein is the only foundation for human beings to be truly free. Law does not override human initiative. To the contrary, Law leads to freedom just as rhythm and beat, tone and cadence lead to Mozart. Ignoring the rules of music results in chaos, not concertos. Ignoring the rules of Natural Law leads to slavery, not salvation.

Freedom is found in knowing and obeying the Truth

Someone else once said that freedom is found in knowing and

obeying the Truth ("You shall know the Truth and the Truth shall set you free"). Maybe this is Hittinger's point. A dog will never be free until she learns to live within the boundaries that are created for her own good. Humans will never experience real liberty until we learn to submit to that immutable Thing that is bigger than self.

This is a lesson reinforced every time I see Blue running in the fields delighted with the freedom she enjoys by obeying her master's voice.

Chapter 37

SINS OF THE RIGHT AND THE LEFT

IN HIS RECENT BOOK, *The Divine Conspiracy,* Dallas Willard talks about what he calls the gospel of sin management. Here he confronts the errors of both Conservatives and Liberals. He challenges the Left and the Right by saying that both have missed the truth of the Gospel by ironically committing the same error: Fixating on sin rather than focusing on personal transformation.

Let me explain.

The Right, Willard contends, holds fast to the gospel of managing one's personal sins. Obsessed with self and legalistic accomplishments, Conservatives tend to withdraw from the corruption of the world and, thus, seek the protection of cloistered communities and exclusive clubs (otherwise known as churches). Just like the self-centered dwarfs in C.S. Lewis' children's stories, we sit in the refuse of our own making and stew about ourselves. It's all about us, you know: Our salvation, our sanctification, our fears and our sins. Say the right prayer. Mouth the right mantra. Run to the altar (the right number of times) and salvation is yours. The world may be damned, but we're not.

Both the Left and the Right have missed the truth of the Gospel by fixating on sin rather than focusing on personal transformation.

The Left, Willard argues, ironically commits the same error but with a slightly different twist. Contrary to popular opinion, Liberals do believe in sin. How else can you explain the indignation of Howard Dean as he railed against the "lies" that led to Iraq, or the anger of Hillary Clinton as she bemoaned a "vast right-wing conspiracy," or the zealous fervor of Al Gore as he preaches the gospel of global warming? Sin is real and there is indeed a lot of it. Just look around, says the Left, at the bourgeois excesses of the Right Wing and you will see all the proof you need.

But here is the difference: For the Liberal it isn't about him and his sin, it is about you and yours. It's about your intolerance, your materialism, your insensitivity, your closed mindedness and your traditional morality. Sin is not measured by objective truths as espoused by the Right. To the contrary, Willard's Liberal darts past any such discussion of divine inspiration with the arrogant confidence of Eden's Serpent to declare, "I don't need anyone else to tell me what sin is or isn't." Social inequities and corporate greed are wrong—not because God says so, but because I do. Public life is the issue, not my private life. Sin is something that others do, and they need to be managed in such a way so that they don't intrude on my self-actualization and my self-esteem, my rights and my choices, my sexuality and my pleasures, and so on and so forth.

So you see, both Conservatives and Liberals are navel gazers. One group looks at its own belly. The other looks at everyone else's. One group is self-centered while the other is sanctimonious. Both focus on gospels of managing sin (either their own or their adversary's) while neither group seems to have any passion for personal piety, for holistic integrity, for selfless regeneration, for public responsibility, for community sacrifice, for character, or for virtue.

It seems to me that we might be missing the bigger message of Jesus: The call for transformation; transformation of individuals as well as culture; transformation of personal life and corporate life; transformation of private as well as public behavior. Maybe Willard is right. Maybe we are so focused on managing the ugliness of sin that we completely miss the redemptive power of the sacred.

Sin's siren has mesmerized us into inaction and hypocrisy where it should have been a warning to seek a "more excellent way."

During this political season, doesn't it strike you as odd that a culture with over 100 million people professing to be followers of Christ can so easily show the world that it is more prone to act like the Donner Party than the Brady Bunch? Time and time again we show our brethren our grisly habit of consuming ourselves as one group rants against personal sins and the other rails against social evils. No solutions, just disgust, diatribes, blame, and bravado.

Willard chastises us. He declares that we (both the Left and the Right) have stared so long at the sun of sin that we are nearly blinded to the way, the truth, and the life of the Savior. Sin's siren has mesmerized us into inaction and hypocrisy where it should have been a warning to seek a "more excellent way."

Managing sin (mine or yours), while a necessary starting point, can never be the end goal. (Isn't this the lesson of the Pharisees?) Anything short of confession, short of forgiveness, short of selfless humility, short of transformation (i.e., short of Christ-likeness) will prove itself to be a morbid fixation on managing the cancer rather than celebrating the cure.

Chapter 38

ORTHODOXY AND ORTHOPRAXY

"Do not give dogs sacred things to eat, nor try to get pigs to dine on pearls. For they will simply walk all over them and turn and take a bite out of you."

MATTHEW 7:6 THE MESSAGE

SINCE I WAS a little boy, I have had a very hard time with this passage of Scripture. It seems so out of place. Where is the kindness of Christ? How does characterizing certain people as pigs and dogs fit with Jesus' message of compassion that pervades almost all His other stories? Over and over again in Scripture we see Jesus reaching out and demonstrating inclusive love. We see him accepting a Samaritan woman whom all the other Jews scorned. He then rescues and forgives a prostitute who is about to be stoned. He even holds up a Gentile (who happens to be a Roman centurion) as a model of faith. And now, all of a sudden, in the middle of the Sermon on the

Mount, Jesus equates some people with "pigs and dogs" and tells us to not give them the pearls of life. How can this be?

The traditional interpretation suggests the following: Some of us have certain wonderful treasures—the pearls of right thinking and right ideas—and we are naturally interested in giving these treasures to everyone around us. Some others, however, are so controlled by their own sin and personal and political delusions that they are not capable of accepting our treasures. They are the pigs and dogs in question. Our job is to tell them the truth. If they won't listen to us, then we are not to waste any more time on them. If they can't see the wisdom of our advice, we should shake the dirt from our feet and move on.

Dallas Willard in his book, *The Divine Conspiracy*, strongly refutes this view. Without any equivocation he states: "It is hard to imagine anything more opposed to the spirit of Jesus than this. So let us be clear once and for all: Jesus is not suggesting that certain classes of people are to be viewed as pigs or dogs. Nor is he saying that we should not give good things and do good deeds to people who might reject or misuse them. In fact, his teaching is precisely the opposite. We are to be like the Father in heaven, who is kind to both the thankful and the evil."

We have a tendency to believe that all we need to do to correct the social problems of our world is to talk.

Willard goes on to explain in a way that finally brings this passage to life for me. He contends: "The problem with the pearls for the pigs is not that the pigs are unworthy. It is not worthiness that is in question here at all but helpfulness. Pigs cannot digest pearls, nor can dogs. And what a picture this is of our efforts to correct and control others by pouring our good [ideas] upon them."

Willard believes Jesus is not being critical of those upon whom the pearl is being pushed, but to the contrary, he is drawing this picture to correct the "pearl pusher"– the one who processes the good stuff—the one who has the right answers. In a crude analogy, Jesus is saying, "Your dog does not see any value in fine jewelry. Are you surprised that, when you try to force feed him pearls, he has no interest?"

I think one of the greatest temptations for all of us is to become pearl pushers. We have a tendency to believe that all we need to do to correct the social problems of our world is to talk. We enter into a monologue of promoting specific ideas, and we think that our words are more than sufficient to convince those around us to change. We know our standards and rules are not bad. In fact they are very good. They are of tremendous value, and we are confident that they are worth a fortune as compared to the poverty that we see in the broken lives of our neighbors. We have the solutions. We couldn't possibly be wrong in "pushing our pearls" on our brothers and sisters, for they surely need them.

But here is the problem: Talking alone is never enough. Pushing ortho-doxy, i.e. right ideas, right thinking, good standards and good rules by telling people what to do, does not change lives. It is akin to trying to

We can't just talk, we must walk the talk.

force a dog or a pig to understand the value of pearls. The outcome is likely to be anger rather than transformation. We will get bit. They will not change.

The message of Jesus buried within the Sermon on the Mount is clear. We do have the truth. The sacred things are real. (Jesus just spent an entire sermon sharing these with us. He wasn't just wasting his breath.) But, as we watch our neighbors make choices that will ultimately destroy their lives, we cannot fall prey to the temptation to simply push our pearls on them. Force feeding through monologue never works. Jesus seems to be showing a different way. Perhaps His intended lesson is this: While cherishing our pearls, we must also value people. We can't just talk, we must walk the talk—we must practice what we preach.

> *As faith without works is dead so are beliefs without behavior.*

As faith without works is dead, so are beliefs without behavior. Yes, orthodoxy is a necessary predicate for transformation, but right ideas are always akin to a lifeless lecture without orthopraxy—the "right practice" of integrity, love, and sacrifice. Transformation almost always follows service, not just sermons.

Chapter 39

ALWAYS WINTER BUT NEVER CHRISTMAS

AS WE COME to the end of another year, I can't help but share one more story from C.S. Lewis' *Chronicles of Narnia*. This is one that many of you already know. It is a scene from *The Lion, the Witch and the Wardrobe*, which was made into a feature film a couple years ago to much acclaim and promotional hype. It is the story of Father Christmas, Lucy, her siblings, and Mr. and Mrs. Beaver as they stand fearful and confused in the cold, frozen tundra of the White Witch's kingdom.

Let me refresh your memory.

The children entered the magic of Narnia through the portal of the professor's wardrobe, and as they did, they found themselves in a winter wonderland of sorts. It is white and cold. The trees have been dusted with frost. The lamppost glows somberly in a windless forest that is blanketed with snow. At first glance, this all seems beautiful—but there is something missing. This land is nearly lifeless, and the few creatures the children do encounter (the fawns, the beavers, etc.) seem fearful, suspicious and nearly paranoid. There is no joy.

By way of explanation, the beavers tell the children that Narnia is under the spell of an evil witch. Everything is pale. Everything is cold. Every moment is governed by fear rather than hope. Every day is as if it is "always winter but never Christmas." This is the dreadful description of life under the witch's rule. There is no hope to wish for and there is no peace to pursue. This is simply a land of despair and defeat.

But this isn't the end of the story. In the midst of Mr. Beaver's description of the evil spell, the children hear sleigh bells ringing in the distance. At first, they are sure this is the sound of the witch's return, and they hide.

But it isn't the witch at all. No, the driver of the sleigh is a great, glad, giant of a man dressed all in red with a white beard flowing down over the breast of his ample robe. It is Father Christmas!

> *"A Merry Christmas! Long live the true King!"*

"I have broken through at last," he says. "She has kept me out for a long time, but her magic is weakening."

Lucy shivers with excitement. "He" is here! And he not only brings presents but he also brings peace and joy. He not only brings hot tea with cream and sugar, but he also offers the comfort of love and the warmth of compassion. He brings music and he brings a message: "Aslan is on the move!" he cries. "A Merry Christmas! Long live the true King!"

Over 2,000 years ago, the world was suffering through a cold dark winter. Civil unrest was rampant in the Middle East and the power of Western Civilization was crumbling under the weight of moral decadence. Rome wielded the sword. Israel picked up stones. Fear killed freedom. Terrorism defeated trust. Even in the midst of the calm of Pax Romana, there seemed to be a cloud of impending doom.

Today, as you watch CNN or read USA Today, you may at times feel the same chill in your bones. You may feel fearful and shiver as you try to shelter yourself from the freezing winds of nightly news. Sudan, Syria, Palestine: Always winter but never Christmas. Iraq, Iran, North Korea: Always winter but never Christmas. "Stimulus" spending and our growing national debt: Always winter but never Christmas. Nuclear proliferation, the threat of terrorism: Always winter but never Christmas. Massive earthquakes, volcanic eruptions and millions of gallons of oil spilling into the Gulf: Always winter but never Christmas.

Remember that light always diminishes darkness, warmth always melts what is cold, and the Son is always stronger than winter.

But in the face of such cold winds, perhaps we would do well to remember the news of long ago when light shone on the hills of Bethlehem and a different Father Christmas arrived singing a new song. "Do not be afraid," He declared in a booming and confident voice. "For behold, I bring you good tidings of great joy." And on that night, hope and love were born anew, winter began to melt away, and Christmas sprang alive in a stable under the stars.

"I have broken through at last," cries Christmas. "She has kept me out for a long time but her magic is weakening. This is a time of love not hatred, giving not getting, goodness not greed. Remember that light always diminishes darkness, warmth always melts what is cold, and the Son is always stronger than winter. Aslan is on the move. For unto you is born this day in the city of David a Savior who is Christ the Lord. He is the light of men. He shines in the darkness and He has made His dwelling place among us. "We have seen his glory, the glory of the One and Only, who came from the Father, full of grace and truth" (John 1:14).

Hilaire Belloc says it well: "Do not, I beseech you, be troubled about the increase of forces already in dissolution. You have mistaken the hour of the night. It is already morning."

"For lo, the winter is past,
The rain is over and gone.
The flowers appear on the earth,
The time of singing has come."

SONG OF SOLOMON 2:11-12

Part Two

A LITTLE "FREEDOM" AND FUN WITH Q AND A

"People need to be reminded more often than they need to be instructed. The real job of every moral teacher is to keep bringing us back, time after time, to the old simple principles which we are all so anxious not to see."

C.S. LEWIS

Chapter 40

SINGLE-ISSUE VOTING: PART ONE

During the 2008 election season, I was involved in a debate with some students who argued that Christian voters need to move beyond their fixation on one or two issues and become more concerned about the "breadth" and "complexity" of human rights and economic justice. Permit me to share the exchange in more detail. You might find it interesting.

Question: Christians need to vote on more issues than just abortion! Why not consider the innocent civilians killed as a result of the Iraq war or all the women and children killed in Darfur and other countries?

Response: I am going to ask you some basic, rhetorical questions. Sometimes this is the most effective tool in trying to resolve deep-seated differences. When we strongly disagree, we often just talk past each other. However, a well-placed question can be of much greater value than dozens of well-worn arguments. So here it goes...

First, when you say that Christians should vote on more than one issue, aren't you being rather presumptuous in implying that single-issue voting is really what "all Christians" do? Isn't it a bit fallacious to lump "all" of any group of people into one big category? I know you are likely saying that you didn't mean "all" Christians but go back and look at the emotion, tone and content of your comments. Your all-inclusive critique of those who disagree with you does come through loud and clear. And, dare I say, your presumption betrays your argument's weakness. Such an indiscriminate casting of the net of criticism falls on some very shallow intellectual waters, in my opinion. I think we should be a bit more disciplined in our logic.

Second, in your argument you hold up abortion and war in juxtaposition. The way you posed your question presupposes that war is wrong. On what premise do you make this claim? Is it because you assume the value of human life? If this is the case, then aren't you admitting that the definition of "humanness" is an objective standard that can never be one group's prerogative to reject or take away? Aren't you basically saying that all human life is an unalienable right endowed by a Creator and never subject to someone else's choice—even in the case of war or abortion?

You see, this is a matter of ontology and epistemology as much as anything. Does life exist and, if so, how do we define or "know" it? If we believe in the objective reality of life and that God is the definer of this reality, then we must never presume to wrestle such "definitions" away from Him and unto ourselves. If the definition of an infant's life is "beyond my pay grade" then would the definition of other important matters likewise be beyond human reason and beyond the responsibilities of my job—i.e., matters such as the end of life and who has the right to determine it, or the quality of life and who has the right to judge it?

Can you see where the momentum of your ideas takes you? If you implicitly diminish the value of life through one means (i.e., abortion), you at the same time minimize the very standards you use to condemn the loss of life through other means (i.e., war). You are sawing off the branch upon which you must sit to make your case in the first place. I believe I have made my point, so I will stop...except for one last thing. If you agree (as you have said) that abortion is a moral tragedy and that "the fewer abortions the better," then aren't you at least, by inference, admitting that the victims of abortion were/are human in the first place? If so, then the entire argument of "choice" must now be abandoned as vacuous because at no time in legal or ethical history has one person's choice ever been rightly elevated above another person's right to live—has it???

Now, I would like to go back to the issue of war. Are you saying that all war is wrong and that total pacifism is your position? If so, great—as long as you are consistent. But if you, like Augustine, believe in a "just war" theology then perhaps it is erroneous to equate the killing of innocent children with the casualties of war. The debate here must start with the question of what is "just" and who determines its definition. Man or God? Political power or divine revelation? Is the killing of millions under the banner of "choice" of any different moral weight than the loss of thousands as a consequence of a war? If you equate the two and say they are both equally evil, then you, by default, should be working as hard to stop one as the other (or maybe harder to stop the one that results in greater quantitative loss). If you minimize one evil to justify your attention given to another, then you subjectively betray your entire argument as nothing but a personal construct that is no better or worse than the "war monger" or despot you protest against.

One last word on the issue of social justice: Is it possible that those on the "Right" might actually treasure justice as much as those on the "Left" and that it is not really a matter of debating values as much as it is a debate of methods? Conservatives might actually cherish freedom, liberty and justice as much as their liberal brothers and sisters. They just might have a different perspective on how to obtain those things.

Now a personal note: I was once much more "progressive" than I appear to be now. I was pro-choice, and I used to be a leading voice for the "you can't legislate morality" crowd. But I don't hold that position anymore for several reasons. First and foremost, I have concluded that it doesn't make any sense. I mean this literally. There is no sense—no logic, no intellectual integrity or moral consistency—in this argument. Legislation, if it is nothing else, is always based on morality. Otherwise there is nothing to legislate and the entire process becomes meaningless. Wilberforce, Wesley and a host of others recognized this. At times these great leaders were indeed dangerously close to being "single-issue voters." John Wesley famously declared that "you must be singular or be damned," and Wilberforce, in like manner, spent decades with near tunnel vision arguing to abolish slavery because he, too, agreed that the definition of personhood was not his to make and was, therefore, not "above his pay grade".

Oh, and by the way, Wilberforce also felt that it was his responsibility to vote for the "restoration of manners"—a return to the humility, modesty and civility that comes from considering the Law and the *Logos* as a singular standard better than the baser proclivities of the human desire, animal instinct and personal passion. Maybe, "single-issue voting" isn't that bad after all.

Chapter 41

SINGLE-ISSUE VOTING: PART 2

A response to an alumnus who argues that Christians need to consider the greater breadth of social justice and human rights and move beyond the issue of homosexual marriage.

Question: Four years ago, you couldn't have convinced me to vote for a Democrat if you had tried. To me, the issue of homosexuality was too big to ignore and to support a candidate that was pro gay marriage was inconceivable. However, I have come to realize that creating laws against these things is not the solution. We have to operate within the framework that we are in. The solution is not to legislate against it. Furthermore, as Christians, we must do such a great job of loving homosexuals that they see the light of Christ through us and want to make good choices.

Response: You have mentioned or implied several issues ranging from legislation to love. Let me try to touch on a few of them with some very brief comments.

First, on the issue of gay marriage, I just have to start by pointing out a major flaw in the logic of the contemporary pro gay agenda. Homosexuality should be a discussion about behavior, pure and simple. It is not about personal identity or human rights. Those who use genetic predisposition or human psychology or physiology as a pretext to justifying homosexual behavior are, in my judgment, employing a *non sequitur* fallacy to the extreme.

A non sequitur is an argument of non-connection where your conclusion does not logically flow from your premise. In laymen's terms, it is a fallacy of "So what?" Let me offer a couple of examples. If my actions are hateful and I cite my family heritage as justification for my hate, your logical response should be, "So what?" If I cheat on my wife and I justify it by saying that all males are genetically predisposed to infidelity, your common sense may lead you to ask, "So what?" If I am angry all the time and I say that biologically I am predisposed to this emotion, you would be well within your rights to respond (or at least think to yourself) "So what?" Isn't it natural for you to respond to such illogical connections by rightly asking, "What does that have to do with anything? So what?"

You see, it is behavior that is in dispute—not one's rights or identity. Minority status has never been about one's proclivities, instincts, desires or consequent actions. To the contrary, it has always been a matter of who you are—not what you do (or what you want to do). Actions can never be the pretext to one's claim of any human rights. Behavioral choices can never be the justification for anyone's claim to minority status. Otherwise, why wouldn't those who practice polygamy, bigamy, inter-species sex, pedophilia, prostitution and a host of other behaviors be as justified in demanding minority status and human rights as any other sub-group?

Next, I would like to respond very briefly to your claim that "We have to operate within the framework that we are in...The solution is not to legislate against it." The simplest way for me to respond to this is to ask this question. Should Wilberforce have responded the same way to the British slave trade? What about Martin Luther King, Jr.—should he just have accepted the given framework of the day and not sought any legislative solutions to the injustices of his time? How about Lincoln and the Emancipation Proclamation? I could go on and on, but I think my point is clear: History is replete with stories of leaders rising up against laws that were unjust and working under the pretext of moral indignation to change such laws through legislative action. Frankly, the argument that you can't legislate morality is a bit empty, because all legislation assumes some common morality. Otherwise, the entire process would be meaningless.

Finally, I would like to comment about what I consider to be an underlying assumption to your argument. You seem to imply that the traditional Christian restrictions on sexual behavior and the Church's enforcement of those restrictions are synonymous with being "unloving." Here is my first blush reaction. Aren't you being just a bit cavalier regarding the principles of physical health, personal responsibility, interpersonal respect and social accountability that have served as the underpinnings of socially acceptable sexual behavior for literally thousands of years?

Human sexual expression has always been weighed on the scales of morality and virtue. Sexual behavior, in all its manifestations, has never been considered to be ethically or legally neutral, even within a secular culture. Agnostics, atheists, Christians and Jews all agree that the use of another person's body for your own sexual fulfillment is wrong—selfish at best and criminal in the extreme. The history of civilization is filled with arguments against sexual immorality. Minimizing the moral weight of such traditional sexual standards doesn't seem to be the best way to elevate your argument to one of love, social justice and civil rights. To the contrary, you might actually find that the time-tested values of sexual restraint as represented in the Judeo-Christian ethic have actually provided the framework for unprecedented love and justice for women and children who were in danger of being subjugated to the passions of the powerful and the prominent. Without such rules and standards, it is not difficult to envision human exploitation and depravity without boundaries. (Turn on the nightly news if you disagree.)

My point is this: If, indeed, you want to argue for love, then isn't the rock of tradition, reason, experience and Scripture worth considering over and above the shifting sands of political fads and popular opinion? On one foundation, you can build a house of justice, dignity, respect and freedom. On the other foundation, you find a crumbling shack of jealousy, depravity, fear and the appalling bondage that comes from the consequences of personal as well as corporate sin.

Chapter 42

USING ABSOLUTES TO REFUTE ABSOLUTES

Here a young man who fancies himself an accomplished post-modern philosopher maintains that the Christian's belief in objective standards of morality is an arrogant imposition by which we Christians try to force our values on the rest of society.

Question: Truth as an "objective absolute" is an arrogant position. This is the problem with you Christians. You always think that you are right. The real enemies of truth are you people who argue for absolutes rather than those of us who contest the constructs of the powerful who want to impose their 'truth' on the rest of us.

Response: First I want to be clear that my response is a critique of your ideas and not an attack of you as a person. It is incredibly important that we remember to honor the dignity of all people as we engage in any debate. Unfortunately, the opposite prevails much too often in our present culture. Disagreement quickly degenerates into yelling, anger and intimidation. These emotional tactics do not lend themselves to rational conclusions. They are distractions, pure and simple, and they only serve to make the attacker feel superior at the expense of his or her more soft-spoken (and often more polite) victim. First Corinthians, as well as basic Socratic logic, clearly condemns such gamesmanship. So, in the following comments I will do my best to stay focused on ideas and their consequences and, thereby, prayerfully flee any temptation to be hurtful, rude or demeaning toward you or others who might disagree with me.

Now with this as context, let me respond to your first point. I have to admit that I smile at bit in reading your statement. You mention that those who claim that there are objective truths are arrogant and that the "real enemies of truth are people who argue for absolutes rather than those who contest such constructs." Here is a question for you to consider: Aren't you arguing for your own absolute in making this claim? Doesn't your own logic assume the very objective standards of measurement that you condemn others for using? The presupposition of your argument, i.e., that you are absolutely right in believing that absolutists are absolutely wrong for believing in absolutes, makes me feel a bit dizzy. Do you see the problem here? You are inadvertently affirming the case for absolutes by using absolute language to refute it.

Next, I have to comment, at least briefly, about the implicit confidence you have in your position. You say, "The problem with Christians is that they always think they are right." Now,

I don't begrudge you the strength of your conviction. In fact, an argument would have little (if any) authority, energy, weight or purpose if it didn't presuppose some degree of accuracy higher than and better than that to which it is juxtaposed. So, I sincerely admire your backbone, but I must at the same time point out a problem imbedded just under the surface of your self-assurance. Here again, your passion to expose the wrongness of someone else's thinking (in this case conservative Christians) simply cannot stand unless the rightness of your own absolute prevails. In other words, aren't you basically saying that you are right in criticizing anyone who thinks they are right, and by doing so, you, by default, have joined the ranks of those you accuse? Your only other position would have to be for you to say that you are wrong in condemning those who always think they are right, but it doesn't appear that you want to go there.

One last point: If absolute truth is nothing but a personal illusion and misplaced arrogance, then all ideas, values and consequent behaviors are merely the product of anthropological constructs. Therefore, it really doesn't matter what a person believes (or for that matter what you and I believe). All that does matter is the political and social power base of a given time and place, and we should all be fine with that—right? If your answer is yes, however, I think we need to go back and reevaluate your original point where you bemoan the "constructs of the powerful who want to impose their 'truth' on the rest of us." Do you see my point? Your position leaves nothing but power (personal or collective) as a basis for you or anyone else to critique and/or challenge someone else's "impositions." As David Horowitz tells us in *Left Illusions,* when we forfeit the absolutes afforded us by boundaries of Truth, we, at the same time, lose all objective measures of what is right and what is wrong. We then suffer the inevitable consequence of being subject to the "rule of the gang" as our final judge, and history tells us that the "gang" is not an arbiter to be trusted.

Chapter 43

PHARISEES AND NONSENSE

This is an exchange with a student arguing that conservative Christians are just like the Pharisees that Jesus condemned.

Question: Why do Conservatives insist on imposing their dead-right and dead-wrong, pharisaical nonsense on the rest of us?

Response: Let me ask you a couple of questions about your comments concerning "dead-right/dead-wrong nonsense." Doesn't your question presuppose that you are "dead right" in condemning those who argue they are "dead right"?! Isn't this a rather self-refuting claim? Doesn't your very premise condemn your own ontology to an epistemological implosion, with your presuppositions collapsing in upon themselves?

Perhaps you have uncomfortably stumbled into the technical definition of non-sense because your position literally makes no sense. As I have said before, righteous indignation directed toward those who always think they are right is akin to saying, "I know that nothing can be known," or, "There absolutely are no absolutes." A little refresher course in the law of non-contradiction might be in order here.

Now let's deal with the matter of Pharisees. The word pharisaical does not (as you imply) reference the belief in objective immutable truth. Rather, it is a condemnation of an attitude of self-righteousness, of arrogance and personal superiority. It connotes a love affair with self—Narcissus gazing with admiration at his own reflection—Carly Simon singing, "You're so vain. I bet you think this song is about you." A Pharisee is one who thinks it's all about him, not all about truth. When someone elevates his/her values and opinions as being superior to God's self-evident truths, that person is indeed a Pharisee. The irony here is that left-of-center progressives tend to commit this error much more boldly than do their right-of-center brothers and sisters.

Conservatives seem to be much more interested in a liberal exchange of ideas than those who proudly call themselves Liberal. Proof: I'm not the one calling on the "politically correct" police to silence the opposition by declaring anything I disagree with as hate-speech. Gnosis and its fastidious tantrum to be liberated from the very self-evident truths that give knowledge any measurability is but one step down the path Robespierre trod as he declared himself to be God and, thereby, handed the guillotine rope to his own executioner.

Chapter 44

CONSERVATIVE OR LEGALISTIC?

This is a brief exchange with a Christian college alumnus who argued that a conservative stance on objective truth and its corresponding moral standards is akin to a return of the legalism of her childhood.

Question: I am concerned that Conservatives tend to call for a return to legalism as the only solution to church apostasy and cultural decay. Legalism isn't the answer.

Response: I agree that legalism is not the solution to apostasy. Both legalism and apostasy are sins that result from the worship of our own intellect rather than the love of God. My own background is not one that embraces legalism at all. This is why I refuse to get caught up in the "worship wars" and other rules-oriented arguments regarding music, dress, denominational peculiarities, etc. My passion is not for legalism and the corresponding self-righteousness that comes with it, but, to the contrary, I have a reverence for "the way, the truth, and the life" and the corresponding humility that follows.

I read once that there are two views of God—the God we want and the God that is. Colleges as well as church movements are prone to create "the gods we want."

The "Word"—the Truth—is the only safeguard we have against such subjective constructs (legalism or liberalism). The Christian college must have as its highest, unshakable goal the pursuit of the "God that is."

Chapter 45

AGNOSTICS AMONG US AND IN US

Here is a simple and honest question about how we can truly "know" anything. Lewis has a great response in The Great Divorce, but perhaps the best response is that of the Roman Centurion who humbly said "Lord, I believe; but help my unbelief."

Question: Isn't agnosticism frankly the most honest position? We really all know that we can't know God. He may be out there but none of us really knows anything about anything other than our own unique experiences and personal realities.

Response: On the question of agnosticism, I personally think what we are dealing with here is pride—pure and simple. When we boil it all down, the agnostic says, "I am the end of all that can be known. I am wiser than those who are so intellectually naïve as to believe in something they can't prove."

Now remember that God laughs at the wisdom of man. Our wisdom is no better than his foolishness. *"We sometimes tend to think we know all we need to know...but sometimes our humble hearts can help us more than our proud minds. We never know enough until we recognize that God alone knows it all"* (1 Corinthians 8:2-3 THE MESSAGE).

C.S. Lewis scolded the agnostic (remember that he was one for the better part of his life) in *The Great Divorce* by saying:

> "Our opinions were not honestly come by. We simply found ourselves in contact with a certain current of ideas and plunged into it because it seemed modern and successful... You know, we just started automatically writing the kind of essays that got good marks and saying the kind of things that won applause. When, in our whole lives, did we honestly face, in solitude, the one question on which all turned: whether after all the Supernatural might not in fact occur? When did we put up one moment's real resistance to the loss of our faith?"

He then goes on:

> "You know that you and I were playing with loaded dice. We didn't want the other to be true. We were afraid of crude Salvationism, afraid of a breach with the spirit of the age, afraid of ridicule, afraid (above all) of real spiritual fears and hopes."

Finally he says:

> "Having allowed oneself [ourselves?] to drift, unresisting, unpraying, accepting every half-conscious solicitation from our desires, we reached a point where we no longer believed the Faith. Just in the same way, a jealous man, drifting and

unresisting, reaches a point at which he believes lies about his best friend."

He concludes:

"Once you were a child. Once you knew what inquiry was for. There was a time when you asked questions because you wanted answers and were glad when you had found them. Become that child again...You have gone far wrong. Thirst was made for water; inquiry for truth."

George MacDonald tells us in the *Curate's Awakening* that, "to know Christ is to do His will. And doing so, we will finally come to know Him. If we want to learn of faith and refute the agnostic within us (and I believe there is one in many, if not all, of us) then we must simply and humbly look to the story of Christ and start by practicing what Jesus says to do. Then, as the Curate says, 'In our attempt to obey the words recorded as His, we will see grandeur beyond the realm of any human invention' and we can boldly 'cast our lot with those of the Crucified.'"

"We know nothing of religion here: we think only of Christ. We know nothing of speculation. Come and see. I will bring you to the Eternal Fact, the Father of all other facthood."
C.S. LEWIS, *THE GREAT DIVORCE*

Chapter 46

WORLDVIEW LANGUAGE IS TOO COGNITIVE

Here is a question from a Christian university faculty member. He is essentially committing the error of so many contemporary academicians who confidently condemn the confidences of those they disagree with. One has to wonder why they even bother to express their view if they don't believe that it is at least in some measure better than the view they are refuting.

Question: Worldview language is an antiquated concept, laden with empiricist/modernist assumptions. Christian education is more about forming love in your gut than about informing your conscious mind?

Response: Very interesting. Upon what definition of "love in the gut" will your school's education be based? Mine? Yours? Your Board's? Who will decide? Will love have an objective definition measured by Natural Law or a universal Tao (C.S. Lewis, Harry Blamires, et al)? Or will this love be subject to the "imagination" of my faculty or yours—or, perhaps, even that of Peter Singer or Ward Churchill?

Lewis' *Abolition of Man* foreshadows this trend of thought in his analogy of "the green book." The Oxford Don warns that we, indeed, do become men without chests when we take the post-modern scalpel of subjective opinions and, thereby, cut from our souls what is objective, immutable and true. This ghastly surgery severs the head from the heart, fact from faith, belief from behavior and leaves us gasping for life that can only be found in the Truth of Christ and the Truth of Scripture. Jesus called it well—We become whitewashed tombs that are superficially attractive but full of nothing but the old bones of spiritual, intellectual and moral decay. One final question: Doesn't the Wesleyan quadrilateral protect us from the false dichotomies of the either/or assumptions of Rational vs. Relational? Doesn't the power of the Wesleyan worldview already honor both?

Chapter 47

IS GOD KNOWABLE?

I was recently asked by a Facebook friend to help him evaluate a YouTube video *Putting Faith in Its Place*. This movie is essentially a rebuttal to the Judeo/Christian view of natural law, common sense, traditional morality and the knowability of God. It uses the analogy of a closed cube to try to prove that we cannot know what is inside the unknowable. Here are a couple excerpts from my comments to my friend that you might also find helpful.

Question: Can we actually know anything about the existence of God? Isn't it impossible to argue for the knowability of something that by definition can't be known?

Answer: Before I presume to offer my own response to your question, I would like to recommend a couple authors with far greater wisdom than me who have made their own honest journey from atheism to faith. I highly recommend you immerse yourself into as much of C.S. Lewis as you can. Read

Mere Christianity (several times). Read *The Great Divorce, Weight of Glory,* and *The Abolition of Man.* In all these classic works, you will find the wisdom of an honest man who is several steps ahead of you on the journey of faith. Lewis' own admission that he was one of the "most reluctant converts in all of England" tells you all that you need to know regarding the difficulty of his trek and the intellectual honesty and the ultimate integrity of his conclusions. You might also consider, Dinesh D'DSouza's *What's So Great About Christianity.* Anything by Os Guinness, Ken Boa, or Francis Schaeffer is going to be excellent. Nancy Pearcy's *Total Truth* is likewise very good. Chuck Colson's *The Faith* as well as *How Now Shall We Live* are seminal publications in my opinion. Harry Blamires' *Christian Mind* and his second book *Post Christian Mind* are, likewise, exceptional.

There is one additional book of which I am fond. It is a great new daily devotional with some truly sound material compiled by Kelly Monroe Kullberg (former Harvard chaplain) entitled *A Faith and Culture Devotional.* I was recently reading a chapter in this book by John Mark Reynolds who is a professor of philosophy at Biola University. This essay by Reynolds is titled "Plato: Lover of Truth, Beauty, and the Good." Here, Dr. Reynolds' basic argument is this: Plato knew that the human heart yearns, hungers, wants, seeks, and longs for truth, justice and RIGHTNESS and these very desires—in and of themselves—are evidence of the existence of some immutable RIGHT (Plato called it Love). Plato says in his book, *Symposium,* that there has to be a greater truth than personal opinions and populist propaganda. Here is a brief dialogue with his mentor Socrates that makes this point:

"Now tell me about love," [Socrates] said, "Is Love the love of nothing or of something?"

"Of something, surely!" [Plato answers].

The point in this exchange between two of the greatest philosophers in recorded history is that human beings have a desire for **ANSWERS**, for JUSTICE and for LOVE—for a BIGGER SOMETHING—for the greater GOOD. As Reynolds says, "The deep longing for justice, beauty and truth must have an end...Plato believed that there was more to the cosmos than empty desire and death." In other words, hunger implies that there is food. Thirst assumes that there is water. Questions are meaningless without the possibility of answers. LOVE cannot exist without an ultimate object of its affection.

In a sense the video *Putting Faith in Its Place* is something akin to a documentary that highlights the existence of hunger to prove there is no such thing as food or one that features a drought to prove there is no such thing as water. Does this make sense? As Pascal said , "The vacuum at the center of every human soul bears the very image of the only THING that can fill this void."

The concept of the closed cube as portrayed in the video is very thought provoking, and, yes, it does remind us that we do "see through the glass darkly" but the very desire to know what is in "the box"—to see more clearly—proves not that the box is empty but, to the contrary, that something must be in the box as the object of our desire. That "something" must be the ultimate ANSWER. Otherwise why care? Why bother? If everything is relative and if there is no such thing as a knowable transcendent truth, then why spend ANY time trying to prove that your argument against my truth is true? Why contend for the rightness of your argument if there is no standard of rightness to prove that I am wrong? The entire presentation of the empty box is built upon the presupposition that the final answer is that there is no answer—a self-refuting claim if ever there was one. Bottom line: The unavoidable pretext for any argument is that someone is right and someone else is wrong, and the producer of *Putting Faith in Its Place* takes 10 minutes to ironically prove this point by essentially saying (with noted pedantic flare) that he is right in condemning those who think they are right.

Frankly, I think the video is quite well done. The writer/producer is very thoughtful and obviously quite bright, but at the end of the video we are left with this question: Which argument measures up? Which position comes closer to the mark? Which one (his, mine or yours) is more right (i.e. closer to truth) than the other? And,in asking all of these questions, we MUST acknowledge a measuring rod outside of those things being measured or we can do no measuring (C.S. Lewis). The video's protest presupposes a jury—its appeal assumes the existence of a Judge. There can be no contest without some rules of engagement, and there must be a referee to make the final call otherwise why would any of us want to play the game or even be spectators. It would be foolishness to go to a Cavs or Celtics game if there isn't some sort of "standard" and "judge" or "referee" to make sense out of the exercise.

In a nutshell my point is this: While doing an excellent job in trying to refute an Objective, Immutable, Unchangeable, Absolute, Reality (i.e. God); the producer of this video has actually proven the opposite. He has to assume there is a *Logos* for there to be logic. He has to assume that there is a Law for there to be lies. He has to assume that there is Righteousness if he is to justify his righteous indignation. He has to assume that he is right if he is to argue that I am wrong. He has to believe in truth for him to claim that someone else's beliefs are false. His words are simply a worthless expense of breath unless these standards of rightness and wrongness come from somewhere OUTSIDE of the temporal human mind (his or mine). His epistemological and ontological nihilism implodes upon itself. It is self-refuting. He would have no energy or desire to prove me wrong if he didn't believe he could PROVE that he is right and that fact may be the best PROOF that God is God and he is not.

Chapter 48

THERE IS A GOD AND ANGER PROVES IT!

In a class on apologetics that I was recently teaching, I tried to make the point that the existence of anger in the form of righteous indignation is ironically one of the strongest proofs of the truth of Jesus Christ and truth of Scripture and ultimately for the existence of God. Here is an excerpt of a question and answer time that followed:

Question: I don't follow your point that "anger" is actually the key that led you to belief in God and ultimately to faith in Christ. Can you tell me again why this is so important in your journey to becoming a Christian?

Answer: Starting at the top of the funnel, I have to ask: Is there a reason to believe in a god? On the broader/bigger questions it seems unavoidable that there must be a "beginner" who is responsible for "beginnings," an "organizer" who is responsible for "order" and an "engineer" who is responsible for "complexity." The explanation of radical Darwinism is absurd to me. Arguing that somehow the "watch" just falls together by chance and starts' ticking without any "watchmaker," just makes no sense. I really believe that had I tried to use such faulty logic to support my doctoral dissertation at Michigan State University, I would have been laughed out of the room. I would have been accused of researcher bias and rightfully so. My committee would have said, "You are obviously side-stepping the data and ignoring the evidence that is contrary to your hypothesis."

While beginnings, order and complexity may infer the existence of a god, these things don't really tell us anything about what that god is like. Obviously, he or it doesn't have to be moral or righteous. He or it could in fact be a distant, amoral or even disinterested and cruel deity: A cosmic sadist who enjoys toying with us? Something like the self-centered gods of the Greeks? Or maybe even the vindictive and demanding god of Islam? Bottom line: Evidence of a creator doesn't necessarily mean he or it is moral and good—right?

So with this all said, what can we say of our assumptions of morality? Of justice? Of righteousness? Of good and of evil? Why do we demand to be treated rightly and why are we angry when we aren't? Where does our indignation come from and why does it matter so much to us? Why do we care?

What I was trying to say in my presentation was this: As ironic as it seems, I believe it is our anger—our quickness to be offended—that seems to be one of the strongest proofs that there must be some *final measure* of morality that justifies and explains our indignation. Otherwise, we really have nothing other than self as a reference point, and arguing with ourselves seems futile to say the least and crazy in the extreme. It would be akin to a lawyer pleading his case with no judge in the bench; or perhaps even worse, like a dog growling at his own reflection in the mirror. Bottom line: If God is not good and just and true and honest—if He is not the author and keeper of righteousness—then what is there to be indignant over and to whom are we pleading our case? How can I explain and justify my anger if there is no ultimate authority to measure its worth? Isn't all indignation simply selfishness if some measure of righteousness bigger than me hasn't been compromised?

All this leads me to the final point I tried to make. If order and complexity point to a god and if indignation and anger point to a standard of righteousness, it seems only reasonable to ask this question: Is there any evidence of a moral standard that is a perfect scale upon which all indignation can be weighed? My conclusion is, Yes! The judge is Jesus. There is nothing in all of human history like the way, the truth and the life that we see in Christ. Like I said of my favorite book, George MacDonald's *The Curate's Awakening*, when we seriously apply the words of Jesus to our daily lives we see "... grandeur beyond the realm of any human invention." Badness is subjective and meaningless unless it is juxtaposed with objective goodness, and there is no example of such goodness other than what we see in Christ. Our anger and indignation only serves to prove that we believe someone has fallen short, and our arguments for justice are really nothing but our subconscious appeals to Him to judge in our favor.

Chapter 49

ANGER, INDIGNATION AND BAD BEHAVIOR

Here is some more good dialogue that stemmed from the classroom exchange regarding the issue that there is a God and anger proves it.

Question: When I try to understand something, I always seek more info and consequently ask lots of questions so here goes: Is there a difference between righteous indignation and conscience? Does one have this indignation only after becoming a Christian or does everyone have it? If everyone possesses it, why does anyone exhibit bad behavior?

Answer: The best way for me to stay on task is to cite your questions one by one and then try to do my best to respond.

1. **"Is there a difference between righteous indignation and conscience?"** The answer is yes. For me, a conscience is that part of man that understands right from wrong. It is our moral IQ, if you will. It is by virtue of my conscience that I know and understand there is an absolute rule or code. Indignation represents my reaction to this code or rule being broken. So for example, my conscience tells me that Truth exists. Indignation is my reaction when someone lies to me. My conscience tells me that animals should be treated humanely. I am righteously indignant when I see my neighbor beating his dog. My conscience tells me that it is wrong to steal. I'm indignant when someone takes things from my office, desk or house without asking. And so on and so forth...

2. **"Does everyone possess a conscience and, if so, how is it developed? Does one have this indignation only after becoming a Christian or does everyone have it?"** There seems to be undeniable evidence that, yes, everyone does have a conscience. In *Mere Christianity*, C.S. Lewis tells how this fact was one of the things that led him from being agnostic to a belief in God. As he looked at the various cultures that spanned the course of human history, he couldn't avoid the evidence of a common moral code that crossed the boundaries of time, geography, race, gender and even religion. Yes, there were some very modest anthropological differences in moral codes, but people by-and-large shared common moral assumptions from tribe to tribe and from age to age. Everyone seemed to also have a common reaction of indignation (i.e. anger) when these codes were violated.

Genesis tells us that what distinguishes man from the rest of creation is that God breathed the breath of life in us (all of us) and thereby created man in His own image. Is it possible that this "breath of life" and "image of God" is indeed moral awareness? Maybe it's "this conscience" that He didn't breathe into a tree, a rock or a cow but did, in fact, breathe into man and woman.

Romans 1 and 2 tells us that "the truth of God is written on every human heart" and that all are "without excuse." Therefore, we all have a moral compass—a conscience—whether we are Christian or not. This fact is born out in our own experience as we see innumerable non-religious people do good simply because it's the right thing to do. Paul, however, also said that because of our stubbornness (whereby we seem to constantly seek to set the terms for the conscience rather than accept the rules and boundaries dictated by God) we have been "given over to a reprobate mind." In other words, we have the intuitive awareness that rules and laws need to exist (that is, we have a conscience). On the other hand, all of us want to "be as God" (Genesis 3) and be in charge of the rules rather than accept them as given by our Creator.

Sidebar: Frankly, this rebellion is being played out in spades right now in the lunacy of our federal government. The White House, Congress and even the Courts want to "be as God." They ignore self-evident truths, and they have been given over to a reprobate mind. They are literally crazy in their arrogance. Yes they have a conscience, but it has been corrupted by hubris (exaggerated pride and self confidence) rather than refined and tempered by humility. Their indignation is without an anchor point. They are angry about injustice, but they are unwilling to admit that the very concept of justice is meaningless unless it is endowed to us by our Creator and not created by us as we struggle for power. They are delusional in quest for godhood.

3. **"If everyone possesses it, why does anyone exhibit bad behavior?"** This comes down to the concept of sin. As stated above, I personally believe that there is irrefutable evidence that we are moral beings and that everyone has a conscience as well as a general understanding of right and wrong. Our propensity to be offended and to thereby feel righteous indignation (to get angry) proves this point. We all intrinsically know the moral boundaries are there, and none of us like it when the boundaries are crossed and we become the victims of those crossing them.

So if we are moral beings, why do we all act immorally? Why do we do bad things? Why do we ourselves cross the boundaries? I think it all boils down to freedom. God created us in "His image" and this by definition means we are free to act as moral beings. We are not like a rock or a chemical compound or a pig or a mule. We are not the sum total of a chemical reaction. We function at a higher level than mere animal instinct. We can *choose* to do something or not do it, and we have intuitive understanding of the moral ramifications of our choices. We are not robots. We are not automatons. We are not mindless bacteria. We are not amoral animals. We are created in "the image of God." This freedom, however, by definition comes with the potential of choosing to do the wrong thing verses the right. And whether we like to admit it or not, one of the most proven facts in all of human history is that we ALL at one time or another choose to do what's wrong. All I have to do is turn on the nightly news to see proof of human sin. And if I don't see it in the news, all I have to do is look in the mirror. "All have sinned and fallen short of the glory of God," as it says in Romans 3:23. Why? The best answer I can give is that we all are guilty of the original sin that took place in the Garden. We all want to be "as God"—to be in charge—to be the ultimate measure of what is right and what is wrong. We all want to justify our indignation. But when all the evidence is in, it seems pretty clear that there indeed is "none righteous no not one," and this is why I have to turn back to the only standard of righteousness and forgiveness that I can find—Jesus Christ.

Chapter 50

GOOD GOD, GOOD PEOPLE AND HELL

And still more from my honest and thoughtful friend. These are questions that we all ask in the privacy of our own prayer closets, and we should all be prepared to give a defense for the faith that lies within.

Question: Perhaps now would be a good time for me to give you my rather simplistic view of religion, and voice some of my doubts/questions. First, I have no doubt that there is a God, and I have no reason to believe that He is not a good and generous God. I believe this god is a "passive" God—He puts us here and nothing we do is predetermined. He simply allows us to fail or succeed. If everything is predetermined, why even bother putting us here unless simply for His amusement? Each of us has a conscience. I'm not exactly sure how it is developed, but I don't have a problem accepting your thoughts on this matter. God is so superior to mere mortals that He put Christ here to have an interface between Him and us. OK so far, but here is where things sort of fall apart for me. If our God is good and generous, what will happen to the huge number of those who do good but are not Christians? It is impossible for me to believe that a good God would simply dismiss those souls.

Answer: I'm sure my feeble attempts to respond to questions that have been plaguing humanity from time immemorial aren't likely to be the end of this (it would be a tad bit presumptuous for me to think otherwise), but let me give it my best shot anyway....

Sidebar: I do think there are times where we all run into a wall constructed of the bricks representing the limits of human reason, and we just have to say "I don't know." Perhaps some of these questions of eternity, etc. lead us head-first into that wall once again as they have time after time in the past. Maybe that's where the phrase "banging your head against a wall" comes into play!!

This all said, I take some comfort in the position of the Greek Orthodox Church where they just say, "We don't know;" and they rest in the "mystery" of God. In this context, the story of the Roman centurion (likely trained and educated in the systems of Greek and Roman logic) who admitted, "Lord, I believe but please help my unbelief" is particularly powerful. I personally think we would all do well to humbly stand with this soldier and even with the blind man at the edge of the Pool of Siloam and admit that we don't know how to answer all the questions—that some things are just beyond our understanding—but that there is one thing we do know: Sight comes from the Savior! "We were once blind but now we see!"

Christ is the reason I can see anything. My only recourse for finding answers to questions that are for me unresolved is to go back to Him as my Teacher and see what He tells me. Like Lewis said, "Christ is either a liar, a lunatic or he is Lord and if he is who he claimed to be (the Lord) then his word on basically everything is the final Word." (Maybe that's why the Gospel of John starts out by telling us that "in the beginning was the Word and the Word was with God and the Word was God?")

So on the question of heaven and hell—there are some things that I just don't understand and where I have to say, "I don't know." In such cases the only way for me to even come a tad bit closer to "getting it" is to go back and read the words of the "Teacher" and "Coach" over and over again and then do my best to understand, believe and obey them. Thus, my affinity for George MacDonald's *The Curates Awakening*—"In my attempt to obey the words recorded as His, I have found grandeur beyond the realm of human invention and I therefore cast my lot with those of the Crucified..."

I do, however, want to make one thing clear. With the admission of my doubts and unanswered questions laid out for all to see, there is one thing I can say with confidence. If there are those out there who have lived lives that need no grace and forgiveness, then I surely know I am not one of them. Like John Newton said, "Amazing grace how sweet the sound that saved a wretch like me. I once was lost but now am found. Was blind but now I see."

So my response to the question of hell is like this—God has not given me the task of serving as judge of those who haven't heard of Christ or of anyone else for that matter. (Thank God—for I would be a lousy judge!) Therefore, when it comes to people who have not heard the Gospel, I can't answer, I have to simply say, "I don't know." But for me personally, there is one thing I do know (or maybe two or three things). I know of my sin and I know that I need to be forgiven and I know there is no viable way for this to happen except through Jesus.

Chapter 51

BORN TO BE WILD—AND GAY?

Here is an exchange concerning the popular argument that homosexuality is not a choice but rather an inherent personal trait much akin to one's race, height, skin tone or other unchosen physical characteristics.

Question: Recently I had a conversation with my neighbor regarding the Wesleyan church. I showed her a hand-out on what Wesleyans' believe on the fact that homosexuality is a choice. My neighbor disagreed. Just yesterday the same topic came up while visiting with three other friends. All three agreed that most homosexual people are born being homosexual. What is your view?

Answer: My personal view of this question on whether or not people are "born" homosexual or not is that in some sense of the word it doesn't matter. Let me explain.

We have to admit that we live in a broken world. All of us are "born" with a sinful nature — with broken bodies, broken attitudes and broken spirits. All of us are born with some compromised aspects of our bodies, personalities and souls. Whether it be physical or mental, none of us come into this world perfect. We all have some limitations we are cursed to accept and wrestle with as we struggle with life.

So, genetic predisposition really doesn't mean that much when it comes to questions of morality and corresponding behavior. For example, some people may be born with a genetic predisposition to be angry. Does that mean they have the right to strike out at others all the time? Does a guy with the "anger gene" have the moral right to hit his children or verbally abuse his spouse? Some folks may be genetically predisposed to pedophilia. Does that give them an excuse to use children for their sexual pleasure? How about racism? If it could be proven that Iranians (or Germans for that matter) are genetically predisposed to hate Jews, would the argument that they are "born this way" justify genocidal actions? You see the "born this way" argument really doesn't work if one believes that we still have the obligation and free will to "behave" morally in spite of our broken world.

Sexual behavior has always been a moral discussion and the measure of right behavior and wrong behavior has never been and can never be grounded in the assumption that we are free to do all the things we were "born to do." We are not animals. We don't just rut about enslaved to uncontrolled instincts. We are moral creatures, which means by definition, that we "don't do" some of the very things we are "born to do."

So I have to conclude that even if someone were to find proof of a gay gene (which, by the way, has been completely misrepresented by the academic elites, the mainline media and most all, others with a libertine agenda—note the blatant falsifications endemic to the Kensey Report for example), it wouldn't matter. Who cares about biological proclivities? You and I are predisposed to do a lot of things that are just simply wrong. Genetic predisposition does not determine what is moral and what is not. If our physiology or chemistry becomes the final measuring rod of right and wrong, then we are left with absolutely no "moral" standards regarding pedophilia, necrophilia, pederasty, bestiality or any other sexual expression. Sex with kids, or sex with kangaroos or sex with a cadaver would all be a matter of personal choice. On what basis would you or anyone else argue that such behaviors are wrong? Frankly, in such a world we would have no moral arguments for or against any action, sexual or otherwise. If personal behaviors are "predetermined" by nature or by nurture, then personal freedom, and any corresponding concepts of morality and personal responsibility, are mute by definition.

Chapter 52

THE PASTOR AND
THE GAY GENE

Here is an example of a fairly aggressive "give and take" on the issue of sexual behavior. This particular exchange was initiated by a Wesleyan pastor who took issue with my previous essay entitled "Born to Be Wild and Gay."

Question: There is a huge difference between the actions of a racist and the actions of a homosexual couple, and to compare the actions of a committed homosexual couple to the actions of a pedophile is disingenuous at best and fear-mongering at worst. Pedophiles are *predators*—their actions harm others. However, a committed homosexual couple does not *necessarily* harm others. Their actions affect themselves and that is a *major* distinction. The unnecessary comparison of homosexuals and pedophiles leads to attitudes in the church that are anti-Christlike. This is not the rhetoric of love or of grace.

Answer: If homosexual behavior is a sin (as it is described in Leviticus and then again in the epistles of Paul as well as implicitly by Christ himself in Revelation) then I am not sure there is a "huge difference" between it and racism, hatred, anger, or other forms of sexual sin such as pedophilia, adultery and whatnot. You seem to be attempting to draw a distinction between a sexual sin that "harms others" and a sexual sin that doesn't. I am not sure I can agree with your epistemology or ontology on this one, and I also have to question your review of Scripture. Christ and Paul both make it clear that a sexual sin (any sexual sin) is not only a compromise of your own body but, also, the compromise of another's and, therefore, all sexual sin "harms others." Thus, the claim that there is a "major distinction" between homosexual sin and other forms of sexual sin seems to fall a bit short in my view. I also must disagree with your point that pedophilia is by definition any more "predatory" than other homosexual or heterosexual sins. I would argue that ALL sexual sin is selfish and therefore by definition, predatory. ALL sexual sin seeks to use another person for one's own fulfillment and satisfaction and, therefore, "preys" on another for the sake of the self.

Finally, I cannot agree it is "anti-Christlike" to point out that it is harmful to compromise basic standards of personal and social health. To remain silent while others hurt themselves does not seem all that loving to me. To the contrary, such silence is akin to enabling people to continue to live a deceptive life that is harmful to themselves, their families and their culture. There are consequences to all ideas, and the consequences of libertine sexuality are quite obvious and quite ugly.

Question: The issue of whether or not homosexuality is genetic is much more significant than you imply. Let's take a different example—schizophrenia. Schizophrenics can do some "immoral" things due to their disorder. Should we damn schizophrenics to hell for these actions? And if a person with Down Syndrome doesn't accept Christ, she will be condemned as well, right? After all, you are saying that genetics is irrelevant. The court system recognizes that there are genetic and mental conditions that mitigate behaviors—someone who is actually, clinically insane is not held criminally responsible for his actions. To say that the discovery of a homosexuality gene wouldn't change anything is going too far.

Answer: The question of "damning" others to hell is not mine to answer. The question of sin, however, has been answered by God's Word. The scenarios you cite above, Schizophrenia, etc. are, I would argue, disingenuous in that you are inappropriately mixing those with illnesses (and compromised rational capacities) with those who are not ill but who simply choose to behave in a given sexual manner. A person's inability to understand right from wrong because of illness is not something to be equated with a person's choice to do wrong rather than right because they feel or believe they were born to do so. With this as context, I don't think it is accurate (or Biblical) to argue that I am "going too far" to say that a genetic predisposition to behave sinfully really doesn't mitigate in any way God's mandate not to do so.

Question: More significant, is the theological side of this debate. Let's assume that in the years to come, there is legitimate scientific proof that homosexuality *is* a genetic thing. In that case, what are we to say about those people and their relationship to God? Did God create them? Absolutely. But wouldn't that mean that God had *created* them in a way that prevented them from following Him? Why would a loving God create a human being with a *physical* predilection toward damnation, a predilection that such a person has no choice about or control over? This is different than "sinful nature," since "sinful nature" is hardly a part of the genetic code. The existence of a homosexual gene—should it ever be proven— would cause some major theological concerns and require some pretty significant rethinking of our understanding of God and of humans.

Answer: Frankly, I am a bit taken aback by this argument. You seem to be saying that people created with any genetic propensity to sin must have thereby been created by God in such a way that prevents them from following Him. You argue that such human beings with a physical predilection toward sin have no choice or control over their behaviors. You finally conclude by contending that "sinful nature" therefore cannot be part of a genetic code. I really don't know how to respond to this than to simply cite the fact that "all of us have sinned and fall short of the glory of God" and that "by one man sin entered the world... etc." It seems quite clear that; First—all of us indeed are born sinful, and second,—all of us have inherited this propensity from our genetic ancestors. We can call it what we will but the propensity to sin is indeed part of our identity as human beings. All of us have physical predispositions to do things that, frankly, we shouldn't do because they are purely and simply wrong. The fact that it is part of our DNA does in no way justify the wrong behavior.

Question: I could say more, but I'll leave it for now. In short, I think you do a disservice to both the church and to the homosexual community when you oversimplify this issue or dismiss the validity of some of the opposing arguments. Like it or not, there are shades of gray on this issue.

Answer: Candidly, I am a bit bewildered as to how calling on all of us to be personally responsible to live godly and holy lives is a disservice to the Wesleyan tradition or the broader Church. As to my comments being a disservice to the homosexual community, again, I don't understand. How could helping a person stop his/her destructive and unhealthy behavior be misunderstood as a disservice? It would seem to me that enabling the same person to continue to harm his body and someone else's would be the greater disservice.

ABOUT THE AUTHOR

Since August of 2002, Everett Piper has served as the president of Oklahoma Wesleyan University. His credentials include a B.A. from Spring Arbor University, a M.A. from Bowling Green State University, and a Ph.D. from Michigan State University.

Dr. Piper's career includes twenty five years of administrative work within the realm of higher education. Prior to becoming the OKWU president, he served in a succession of vice presidential roles in the areas of Student Development, Institutional Advancement, Enrollment Services, and Capital Projects. Other leadership roles have included the Chairman of the Bartlesville Chamber of Commerce, member of the Arvest Bank Advisory Board, member of the Bartlesville Symphony Orchestra Board of Trustees, member of the General Board of the Wesleyan Church of North America, former president of the Association for Christians in Student Development, Adjunct Scholar for the Oklahoma Council for Public Affairs, and a current member of the Council for National Policy. Dr. Piper contributes regularly as a writer for the *Examiner Enterprise*, Chuck Colson's *BreakPoint* magazine, Crosswalk.com, Politicalmavens.com as well as the Oklahoma Council for Public Affairs' *Perspectives* magazine.

Dr. Piper speaks boldly and unapologetically on issues such as natural law, unalienable rights, self-evident truths, and the unavoidable consequences of ideas on personal, political, community and corporate wellbeing. He challenges his academic and political peers for what he calls their "fallacious Orwellian duplicity" of "intolerant tolerance." His commentary rhetorically confronts the reader and listener to consider issues such as freedom, justice, common sense, human dignity, sexual responsibility and moral objectivity. Piper is specifically passionate in arguing that postmodern political correctness is really nothing more than an unvarnished ploy to consolidate power among society's elites and to, thus, restrict the individual freedoms and rights of the general public. He claims that without an objective moral standard (above and beyond the subjective feelings and wishes of those in power) there is no freedom, there is no justice, and there is no liberty. Opinion as the final measure of right and wrong always leads to the rise of the "rule of the gang" or "the tyranny of one."

Dr. Piper and his wife of 25 years, Marci have two sons, Seth (17) and Cobi (14).